JESUS - LIGHT
of the
WORLD

By
Father Robert J. Fox

Cover Design and Illustration by
Sister Mary Loretta, V.H.M.

Published by
Fatima Family Apostolate
Box 55, Redfield, SD 57469

NIHIL OBSTAT:
Reverend John T. Folda, S.T.L.
Censor Librorum

IMPRIMATUR:
✠ Most Reverend Fabian W. Bruskewitz, D.D., S.T.D.
Bishop of Lincoln

July 14, 1997

The **Nihil Obstat** and **Imprimatur** are a declaration that a book or pamphlet is considered free from doctrinal or moral error. No implication is contained therein that those who have granted the NIHIL OBSTAT and IMPRIMATUR agree with the contents, opinions, or statements expressed.

ACKNOWLEDGEMENTS

Excerpts from the text of the Confraternity Edition of the Holy Bible contained in this book, *Catholic Truth for Youth*, are reproduced by permission of The Confraternity of Christian Doctrine, Washington, D.C., Copyright owner. All rights reserved.

Excerpts from the following documents are printed with permission from the United States Catholic Conference: *General Catechetical Directory, Behold Your Mother, Basic Teachings for Catholic Religious Education* and *Morialis Cultus*. The complete documents are available from:

United States Catholic Conference Publications Office
1312 Massachusetts Ave., N.W.
Washington, DC 20005

Appreciation is extended to the World Apostolate of Fatima for permission to reprint from my earlier book, *Catholic Truth for Youth*. The illustrations were copyrighted by The Blue Army in 1978, and are reprinted with permission. ISBN: 09265429

Appreciation is given to Fr. Rossi Severo, Consolata Missionaries, of Fatima, Portugal, for permission to use the cover picture of the Sacred Heart of Jesus.

Printed by Park Press Quality Printing Inc. Waite Park, MN 56387

DEDICATION

This book is dedicated to the Sacred Heart of Jesus and the Immaculate Heart of Mary. It honors in a special way all the angels and saints in heaven as well as those "hidden" saints on earth who have contributed to this book by their prayers, work and sacrifices.

May Our Lady of Fatima teach us to love her Divine Son and share in the dispositions of her own Pure Heart.

Father Robert J. Fox

For additional copies of this book write:
FATIMA FAMILY APOSTOLATE
Box 55, Redfield, SD 57469
or Fax 1-605-472-4113.

CONTENTS

PREFACE

Dear Friend:

It is my prayer that this catechism, *Jesus - Light of the World*, will bring you to a personal relationship with our Lord and Savior, Jesus Christ. May this catechism enlighten you about the great love that God has for you as an individual. May you be led to a life of prayer in union with Jesus Christ, especially in the Holy Eucharist, which must always be the end of any study of our holy Catholic faith.

While this book is not primarily a devotional book, it does contain truths about the divine Person made man whom each one of us must know and love to be happy here on this earth – a knowledge and love we must live to get to heaven. Catholic doctrines are just that – truths about the Person we must love.

Jesus said, "I am the way, and the truth, and the life" (Jn 14:6). The Apostle of love, St. John, opens his account of the Holy Gospel of Jesus Christ by saying, "In him was life, and the life was the light of men" (1 Jn 5). Two times the same Apostle quotes our divine Lord saying, "I am the light of the world" (Jn 8:12; 9:5).

Young Catholics today have the opportunity of becoming the most enlightened Catholics in the 2000-year history of the Catholic Church. Why? Because now the Catholic world has a major Catechism which was approved by Pope John Paul II in the Apostolic Constitution, *Fidei Depositum*, (October 11, 1992) and ordered to be published for use throughout the entire world under the title *Catechism of the Catholic Church*. It is available in English and the other languages of the world.

That Catechism, said the Pope, was given "that it may be a sure and authentic reference text for teaching Catholic doctrine and particularly for preparing local catechisms."

Jesus - Light of the World is presented to you as being in harmony with the universal *Catechism*. The more initial and more simple portions of each lesson which can be easily understood formerly appeared under the title: "Catholic Truth for Youth" and was scrutinized in this edition to be in harmony with the teachings of the *Catechism of the Catholic Church*.

Each of the 33 lessons presents additional material, "For Older Students." These lesson sections are a summary of the same truths which the universal Catechism teaches. They are found here in a somewhat simplified manner from what the universal *Catechism* teaches on the same subjects.

Pope John Paul II said the *Catechism of the Catholic Church* "is a statement of the Church's faith and of Catholic doctrine, attested to or illuminated by Sacred Scripture, the Apostolic Tradition, and the Church's Magisterium." He added: "I declare it to be a sure norm for teaching the faith..."

Students who master the entire contents of *Jesus - Light of the World* should then be prepared to use the universal *Catechism* itself which should be in the library of every Catholic home, and a reference tool for every teacher of the Catholic religion.

Father Robert J. Fox

INTRODUCTION

Jesus – Light of the World was written to help young Catholics know, love and live their holy faith.

It first presents a concise summary of the basic doctrines of faith and morals of the Catholic Church in simple, interesting language.

Each of the 33 lessons in this book develops an important topic of faith. There are five major sections in each lesson:

1. Doctrinal Instruction in simple language
2. Doctrinal Instruction for older students
3. Review Questions with answers
4. Discussion Questions
5. Points for Parents and Teachers

Younger Students

Junior High School students should be able to handle all the material of each lesson except for that designated for older students. Intermediate students would need special help from parents and teachers.

Parents and teachers may simplify or expand the concepts and vocabulary to suit the particular needs, interests, age or ability of the individual student or group.

Older Students

Reference numbers from the *Catechism of the Catholic Church* at the end of the material "For Older Students" indicate where the same subject is developed at greater length and depth in the official Catechism for the universal Church with more Bible references often listed.

The "Questions to be answered" at the end of this second part of each lessons are intended only for more advanced students such as high schoolers and beyond.

The use of *Jesus - Light of the World* by older students and even adults will enable them to discover how to use the *Catechism of the Catholic Church* promulgated by Pope John Paul II on October 11, 1992, and intended as a guide for the writing of future catechisms. This was the first Catechism issued for the universal Church in more than 400 years since the *Catechism of the Council of Trent*, or *Roman Catechism*, was issued after the Protestant Reformation of the early 16th century.

Older students are advised to study well all the material of each lesson. Having first comprehended those portions of each lesson which use more simple language and concepts they will then be enabled to comprehend more easily the advanced material.

Review Questions

The Review Questions in part three focus the reader's attention on the important concepts of the lesson and sometimes provide additional information. Although the review is presented in "question-answer' form, it is recommended that students express the answers in their own words. (They may do this either verbally or in writing.) In those cases where memorization of certain answers is the most effective and practical method to be used, children should understand all they memorize.

Discussion Questions

Thought-provoking questions are provided in the fourth part of each lesson. These comprehensive questions review the salient points present in the doctrine text. They will help students explain and discuss their faith intelligently.

These questions serve as excellent guides for silent, independent reading because all the answers can be found in the lesson. They also provide an interesting review or "post-reading' group activity.

The "Questions to be answered" for older students are based on the more advanced material of each lesson which summarizes teachings on the subject from the universal Catechism.

Points for Parents and Teachers

This part of each lesson is short and to the point. The author simply outlines the goals of the lesson and notes positive aspects which parents and teachers should stress as well as dangers which should be avoided.

Reference is often made to authoritative documents containing important information adults should understand, especially those teaching youth. It is advised that parents and teachers read this section first in order to gain the proper overall view of the lesson.

Catechism of the Catholic Church

Parents and teachers now have a valuable tool for deeper resources in the official universal catechism of the Church. All the subjects dealt with in *Jesus - Light of the World* are to be found in the *Catechism of the Catholic Church* with reference numbers indicated at the end of the "For Older Students" material.

Use of the Bible

The universal Catechism gives countless biblical references which can be located to discover how the Word of God teaches the truths of the doctrines of Catholicism. *Jesus - Light of the World* offers some Biblical references. The student or teacher who desires more abundant exposure to the Bible will easily find in the *Catechism of the Catholic Church* in the footnotes of its pages even more biblical references than are given in the catechism for students.

Parents and teachers are encouraged to require students to discover how to locate biblical texts. They should then read directly from the Bible at least some material that substantiates especially those doctrines so crucial and central to Catholic life, such as the Holy Eucharist as sacrifice and the seven sacraments. Students required to take their Bible in hand and read John 20:19-25 relating how Jesus gave His first priests the power to forgive sins in His name will have a lasting effect.

For People of All Ages

Jesus - Light of the World is meant for ALL youth. Adults will gain much from reading and studying it.

The parts of this catechism with more simple language have already been used by many thousands of youth successfully. Even students of intermediate age have been able to use the parts not designated for older students when they were given special guidance by parents and other teachers.

Concentric Method

The concentric approach to the study of our holy Catholic faith has been highly recommended as essential to grasping the faith gradually more in depth. This means not simple repetition but each time the subject is studied it is dealt with in greater depth, especially as one advances in age.

There are three levels of presentation of subject matter available through the use of *Jesus - Light of the World*, each one of greater depth. Two levels are clearly presented in this book. The third would be to use the universal Catechism itself in conjunction with this present volume, discovering in this way where the doctrines are dealt with in the Church's official Catechism intended to assist Pastors and Catechists throughout the world. The older student should be capable of reading that material after comprehending all that is in the lessons of *Jesus - Light of the World*.

As students advance in age this book may be used a second or third time when sufficient time has elapsed since it was initially introduced. By supplementing the basic content with enrichment units and other activities, parents and teachers would be able to hold the interest of students, at the same time expanding their understanding of it.

Use in Home, School and Parish

Jesus - Light of the World is a versatile book suitable for religious instruction in the home school, parish or youth Prayer Cell Programs because its content is "Catholic" or "universal." Beautiful illustrations are used profusely throughout the text. In addition to being inspirational, this religious art also helps the student understand and remember the lessons.

Acknowledgments

Although it is impossible to list the names of all the people who have contributed to this book by their prayers, sacrifices and efforts, the author wishes to thank each one. Special mention is made to Rev. Msgr. William E. Maguire, S.T.D., Reviewer of the Diocese of Trenton, N.J., who with pastoral zeal and concern, made a careful critique of this book, under the title "Catholic Truth for Youth" when it first appeared to make sure it was loyal to the faith and morals of the Catholic Church and in addition, made other constructive suggestions that enhanced its general effectiveness.

The part to each lesson, "For Older Students," was later added in the 1997 edition to incorporate the use of the *Catechism of the Catholic Church* while the original text was carefully scrutinized to be in harmony with this universal Catechism.

LESSON 1
GOD AND RELIGION

God is the all-powerful, all-knowing, all-loving Supreme Being Who created heaven and earth and each one of us. To love Him, we must know Him.

If God should forget anyone, even for a moment, that person would immediately return to the nothingness from which he was made. But God will never forget a single person. Each human being will exist forever because he possesses an immortal soul.

If God stopped thinking of us for one second, He would not be God. To be God means to be the Supreme Being Who made all things and keeps them in existence every moment by infinite power and love.

Each person is more important to God than the whole world and everything in it. It is true that God loves the world, but each man means more to Him than all the stars, planets, animals, plants—all visible creation.

Material things (like chairs, houses, desks, etc.) are made up of millions of atoms. Every atom is so tiny it can only be seen with the aid of an electron microscope, yet each has many parts and is in itself a little universe.

Now, if God made, knows, sees and keeps in existence every atom with all its parts—and He does—how much more

*God is the Supreme Being Who made
all things and keeps them in existence.*

does He know, see and keep in existence His children whom He created and loves.

If one were to go to the depths of the earth or heights of the sky, God would be there. But He is also where you are now and where this lesson is being written. This is just another way of saying God is everywhere at the same time. He exists in all creation which He sustains at every moment.

This lesson will be read by many people at different times and at different places, yet at this moment God sees each person as he will read it, as well as the author who is now writing it. In fact, God has seen this from all eternity, for each person has always existed in His mind. God has, indeed, known and loved us everlastingly. He always was, is and will be.

God is the Supreme Spirit Who is everywhere. Although we cannot see Him with our human eyes, He can and does see us. In fact, God not only sees everything but He knows everything, even our most hidden and secret thoughts, words and actions.

There is only one God because only one Being can be infinite. Think about this. Only ONE Being can be almighty and contain all beauty, truth, goodness, knowledge and power. If God lacked some quality which another being possessed, He would not be God. To be God means to have everything without limit.

Religion is the relationship between God and man. Through it man tries to know, love, serve and obey God. Religion also means worshiping God in special ways and at special times. This is the only way man can fulfill the purpose for which he was created. This is the only way he can be happy in this world and in the next.

REVIEW QUESTIONS

1. Who is God?

God is a Spirit, infinitely perfect. We cannot see Him because He is invisible to our bodily eyes. God is everywhere. He made all things out of nothing and keeps them in existence at every moment. God is all-good and loving.

2. What is religion?

Religion is the bond between God and man. Through it man strives to know, love and serve God.

The Catholic Christian Religion is supernatural. It has been revealed by God through His Son, Jesus Christ. Thus, it came from the one true God and is directed back to Him.

DISCUSSION QUESTIONS

1. Using your own words, explain Who God is.

2. How can God see the author as he writes this lesson and you as you read and discuss it all at the same time?

3. Will God ever forget any of His creatures? Explain.

4. Is it possible for anyone to keep a secret from God? Explain.

5. Is there any place where one could hide from God? Explain.

6. Could there be more than one God? Explain.

7. Could one be perfectly happy without God? Explain.

FOR OLDER STUDENTS

It is written in the heart of man to desire God. God is always drawing man to Himself. Man is always searching for God. Man especially bears a resemblance to God and God transcends all creatures including man. By nature man is a religious being and can fully live his life only by being bonded with God. Listening to the voice of conscience, man can realize the existence of God. The one true God can be known from His works and by human reason. God in His love for mankind revealed Himself to us and we have His revelation recorded in Sacred Scripture and in the teachings of His Church.

Catechism of the Catholic Church: 26-43.

Bible References: Genesis 1:27; Wisdom 13:5 43; Acts 17:26-28; Ps 105.

Questions to answer:

1. Explain: "Man by nature is a religious being."
2. Why does man especially bear a resemblance to God?
3. How is man always searching for God?

●●●

POINTS FOR PARENTS AND TEACHERS

In helping young Catholics with this lesson, parents and teachers must make a clear distinction between what is natural and what is supernatural.

Man can give homage to God even when he does not have the help of divine revelation. Natural insights and experiences can lead to a religion that is natural and not supernatural. Therefore, it is necessary that children understand concepts like, "supernatural, spirit, infinite, eternity, etc." Educators who carefully explain the meaning of words are using good teaching techniques. Rote memorization without understanding is ineffective.

The lessons in this book have been written to instruct and motivate youth to know, love and live their holy Catholic Faith.

●●●

God created heaven and earth and all things by His almighty power. His chief creatures are angels and men.

Because God is infinitely perfect and happy in Himself, He did not need man. Yet out of love God created man, forming him in His own image and likeness.

The Bible teaches that Adam and Eve were the first two people on earth. In 1950, Pope Pius XII wrote a letter to the world in which he stated that Catholics may not believe some men on earth came from another race after Adam or that Adam stood for a group of men.

God is the highest or Supreme Spirit Who always was and always will be. Long before God made man, He created lesser spirits than Himself called angels. Angels are pure spirits without bodies who possess great understanding, power and free will.

God tested the angels so they could prove their love by freely choosing to know and serve Him. Some angels (called fallen angels, bad angels or devils) were cast out of heaven after they sinned. Their leader, Lucifer, whose name means "light-bearer," became Satan, the prince of darkness. St. Michael the Archangel led the good angels who remained faithful to God.

Our first parents, Adam and Eve, were also given a test so that they, too, could freely choose to love and obey God. The

Angels are pure spirits without bodies
who possess great understanding,
power and free will.

devil tempted Eve; and she, in turn, led Adam into sin. The Bible states that our first parents disobeyed God by eating fruit from the tree of good and evil.

Before Adam and Eve sinned, they enjoyed many special gifts from God: sanctifying grace, the right to heaven, happiness in the Garden of Paradise, great knowledge, freedom from suffering and death, and control of their passions. After they disobeyed God, our first parents lost these gifts for themselves and for their descendants. Because Adam sinned, men are born without grace and inherit his punishment just as they would have inherited his special gifts had he been obedient to God.

The "first" or original sin of the human race was committed by Adam and Eve. It is passed down from Adam to all men. The only human person who was preserved from original sin was the Blessed Virgin Mary, the Mother of Jesus.

Pope Pius XII addressed the world about the doctrine of original sin. He said: "Original sin is the result of a sin committed, in actual historical fact, by an individual man named Adam...it is a quality native to all of us, only because it has been handed down by descent from him" (cf. Romans 5: 12-19).

Since all men inherit original sin from the father of the human race, they are born without grace as creatures of God and children of their natural parents. However, at Baptism they are restored to grace and become God's children by adoption.

Because of original sin, men are inclined to evil. Satan and other evil spirits continually try to cause men to sin. On the other hand, the good angels (particularly each person's own special Guardian Angel) try to help men obey God and live in His grace.

The sin of the bad angels was very great because they possessed tremendous intellects and wills. God gave the angels only one opportunity to choose or reject Him. Such was not the case with man. After Adam sinned, God promised to send a Redeemer Who would make satisfaction for original sin and all the sins which the children of Adam and Eve would commit throughout the ages of time.

Although men are inclined to evil and must suffer pain, death and the loss of many special gifts originally given to our first parents by God, they still may live in hope. God kept His word and, in time, sent His only-begotten Son Who redeemed the world and won back grace and the right to heaven for all mankind.

REVIEW QUESTIONS

1. What are angels?

Angels are pure spirits without bodies who possess understanding and free will. The good angels remained faithful to God and thus enjoy His presence forever in heaven.

2. What do the good angels do?

The good angels know, love, adore and serve God Whom they see. Sometimes they act as God's messengers to men. The good angels protect us from harm, inspire us to be good and help us by their prayers. Each person has his own Guardian Angel who helps him in a special way.

DISCUSSION QUESTIONS

1. What are the two chief creatures of God?
2. Recite the Guardian Angel Prayer. Angel of God, my guardian dear, To whom His love commits me here, Ever this day be at my side, To light and guard, to rule and guide. Amen. (Partial Indulgence.)
3. What are the fallen angels called?
4. Why do devils try to lead men into sin?
5. What did our first parents, Adam and Eve, lose for themselves and for their descendants by their sin against God?
6. What did Pope Pius XII write about Adam in his 1950 letter to the world?
7. Explain what the following means: "Man inherits original sin from Adam."
8. Why weren't the fallen angels given a second chance after they sinned?
9. What promise of hope did God make to Adam and Eve before they were driven from Paradise?

●●●

FOR OLDER STUDENTS

A truth of faith is that there are beings which exist which are completely spiritual and have no physical bodies. The Bible calls these spirits angels of heaven.

At the center of the angelic world is Jesus Christ. Angels have existed as long as creation and have always had a role in announcing salvation to mankind. Their work continues in the life of the Church.

The fall of some of the angels represents an irrevocable sin. Fallen angels, devils, can never repent. Therefore they can never be forgiven. It was their own free decision and they can never change their mind away from sin.

No angel has ever directly experienced the mercy of God. Fallen angels hate the mercy of God. The good holy angels are in awe at God's mercy bestowed upon mankind. That God became man in Jesus Christ and died on the cross for His sinful brothers and sisters is a mystery which the good holy angels love and cherish. The holy angels discover more about the mercy of God in their relationship to mankind. This is why the Bible tells us that there will be joy in heaven among the angels over one repentant sinner "more than over ninety-nine just who have no need of repentance" (Lk 15:7).

The reality of sin and its great evil was only gradually understood by mankind as God gave more and more Revelation. Only with the death and Resurrection of Jesus Christ does mankind come to the full meaning of the story of the creation and fall of man which was first told in the book of Genesis of the Bible. The New Testament of the Bible often refers back to that first part of the Bible where the devil tempted man to fall.

Catechism of the Catholic Church: 325- 329; 331- 336; 385 395; 391-93, 414.

Bible: Genesis Chapters 1 to 5; Gen 3:24; 2 Thess 2:7; 1 Tim 3:16; Rom 5:20; 12-21; 8:28 Lk 11:21-22; Jn 8:44; 16:11; Mt 4:1-11; 1 Jn 3:8; Gen 3:1-5; 1 Jn 3:8; Jn 8:44 Wis 2:24; Jn 8:44; Rev 12:9 Pet 2:4. Ps 115:16; Mt 18:10. Mt. 1:20; Mt. 25:31; Col 1:16; Heb 1:14; Heb 1:6; Acts 1:10-11; 5:18-20; 7:53; l Kings 19:5 Mk 16:5-7.

Questions to answer:

1. Name at least 2 times when angels played a role in announcing salvation to mankind.
2. How long have angels existed? Did God create angels or man and woman first?
3. Why was the sin of the angels irrevocable?
4. Why are the good holy angels in awe at the mercy of God?

Each person has his own Guardian Angel
who helps him in a special way.

POINTS FOR PARENTS AND TEACHERS

In teaching this lesson, the following points should be emphasized:

1. Angels are "real," not "imaginary," spirits who form part of God's family.
2. Angels are lifetime guardians and friends of men. Their interest and protection is not confined to childhood days only.
3. Angels were essentially made to know, love and serve God. They find their happiness and fulfillment in this.

The Church teaches that Adam and Eve were historical people. Young Catholics should understand this truth. Pope Pius XII stated: "Original sin is the result of a sin committed, in actual historical fact, by an individual man named Adam..." Students must also realize that man inherits original sin and suffers its consequences, even though Jesus Christ has redeemed the human race.

Catholics must reject all false modernistic teachings that deny the historicity of our first parents, original sin, etc. Such teachings have been and continue to be rejected by the one, holy, Catholic and Apostolic Church.

●●●

LESSON 3
CHRISTIANS ARE
CHILDREN OF THE PROMISE

When our first parents, Adam and Eve, sinned, they lost grace and the right to heaven for themselves and all men. However, before they were driven from the Garden of Paradise, God promised He would send a Redeemer Who would regain these special gifts for mankind.

But sin is so terrible and grace so great that not even the sacrifices and penances of all men would be enough to redeem the world. Therefore, God gave us Someone, His only-begotten Son, Who could and did make sufficient satisfaction for sin. The God-Man, Jesus Christ, became the new Head of the human race so that as all men died in sin by the first Adam, all would be able to rise in grace by the new Adam.

When God made His great promise, He told the devil, "I will put enmity between you and the woman, between your seed and her seed; he shall crush your head, and you shall lie in wait for his heel" (Genesis 3:15).

The woman Mary had a Child, an Offspring, Who was Jesus Christ. That is why the devil hates her. Knowing that Jesus' Mother always leads men to her Divine Son, Who crushes his head, the devil does all that he can to keep us from knowing and loving Jesus and Mary.

Thus, It was Jesus Who enabled all men to become His brothers and sisters and children of God. He, as Savior, truly

*Jesus enabled all men
to become His brothers and sisters
and children of God.*

overcame darkness and is the Light of the world. Although Jesus Christ is Man, He is also God. We profess this every Sunday at Mass when we say that Jesus is "...God from God, Light from Light, true God from true God... "

God alone is infinite or without limit. Because Jesus Christ is God, He was able to make infinite satisfaction for sin. We call Jesus our Redeemer because He paid the price of our salvation by dying on the Cross and shedding His Precious Blood for men. Throughout time, Christ perpetuates His Sacrifice on Calvary at every Holy Mass. After His resurrection, Our Lord's five glorious wounds remained. Shining like precious diamonds, they remind us of the cost of our redemption.

Each human being is but one person. However, in the ONE God, there are THREE Divine Persons, the Father, the Son and the Holy Spirit. Each Person of the Blessed Trinity is God and each is perfectly equal to the other.

The Trinity is a mystery which cannot be fully understood. It is sometimes likened to a triangle made up of three equal sides. As the triangle is one, so the Trinity is one. Yet the triangle is made up of three individual, equal sides and the Trinity is made up of three distinct, equal Persons: God the Father, God the Son and God the Holy Spirit.

Jesus Christ is truly God because He is the Son. Only He, the Second Person of the Blessed Trinity (not God the Father or God the Holy Spirit), took the nature of man and became the God-Man, Who is Our Lord, Savior and Redeemer.

Jesus Christ is God's promise to mankind fulfilled. It is only through Him that Christians become "children of the promise."

REVIEW QUESTIONS

1. How many Persons are there in God?

There are three Persons in God:

    1. God the Father.
    2. God the Son.
    3. God the Holy Spirit.

The three Persons in one God are called the Blessed Trinity.

2. Which of the three Persons in one God became Man?

God the Son, the Second Person of the Blessed Trinity, became Man. As Man, God the Son is called "Jesus Christ."

Jesus Christ, the God-Man,
made infinite satisfaction for the sins
of men.... He perpetuates His sacrifice
on Calvary at each Holy Mass.

3. Is Jesus Christ true God?

Yes, Jesus Christ is true God and true Man.

DISCUSSION QUESTIONS

1. Why could Jesus alone offer sufficient reparation for sin and thus redeem mankind when all men together could never do this?

2. Why is Jesus called the "new Adam"?

3. Why does the devil hate Mary so much?

4. Why is Jesus called our Redeemer?

5. How did Jesus reopen the gates of heaven for mankind?

6. What marks still remain on Jesus' body in heaven to remind us that He is our Redeemer?

7. Which of the three Persons in the one God became our Savior: God the Father, God the Son or God the Holy Spirit?

FOR OLDER STUDENTS

As a result of original sin inherited from Adam we enter the world deprived of original holiness and justice. Yet human nature is not totally corrupted. It is wounded in its natural powers. This means we are subject to ignorance, suffering, and death and have inclinations to evil which are called "concupiscence." While baptism imparts the grace of Jesus Christ, erases original sin, turns the person back toward God, yet, the consequences of human nature weakened by the fall remain and we must do battle with inclinations toward sin throughout life. Jesus required faith and baptism for the forgiveness of sin. Jesus Himself said baptism is necessary for salvation. (Jn3:5). A person later in life who makes a profession of faith while receiving Baptism is cleansed so fully and completely that absolutely nothing of sin remains, nor is there any vestige or penalty due to forgiven sin remaining. The weakness of human nature, however remains.

Baptism is the first of the sacraments of Christian initiation which lays the foundation of every Christian's life, making one for the first time a "partaker of the divine nature," an heir with Jesus Christ, a temple of the Holy Spirit. Confirmation and the Eucharist are sacraments of initiation after Baptism which increase divine life in the soul and advance one toward the perfection of charity.

Baptism is the door to all the other sacraments of the Church as it not only frees us from sin but through it we are reborn as children of God and become members of Jesus Christ. This sacrament is called "the washing of regeneration and renewal by the Holy Spirit," Baptism makes one "a new creature," in Christ and an adopted son of God. The ordinary ministers of Baptism are the bishop, priest and deacon. In case of necessity, anyone can baptize. Even someone not baptized can baptize if they have the right intention to do what the Church does when she baptizes. The person must use the Trinitarian baptismal formula at the same time water is poured, namely, "I baptize you in the Name of the Father, and of the Son, and of the Holy Spirit."

The person who has been baptized receives the Word, "the true light that enlightens every man," (Jn 1:9; 1 Thess 5:5; Heb 10:32; Eph 5:8). The Church has always taught that those who die for the faith without the opportunity of Baptism by water are baptized in their death for and with Christ. It is called Baptism of blood.

Catechumens who are repentant of their sins and love God

but who die having firmly desired Baptism but never had the opportunity receive Baptism of desire. Those who never receive any Christian instructions and remain ignorant of the Gospel of Jesus Christ and His Church, through no fault of their own, but during life seek truth and the will of God can be saved. It may be supposed that these would have desired Baptism explicitly had they known it was necessary for salvation.

The Church commends the souls of children to the mercy of God who die without Baptism. We know that the infinite mercy of God desires the salvation of all. The Church hopes there is a way of salvation for these children. Some devout Catholics frequently make acts of desire for children who die without Baptism, such as those who are aborted.

The Church instructs that parents, sponsors, and the pastor are to see that a name is not given a child at baptism which is foreign to Christian sentiment. The sacrament is conferred "in the name of the Blessed Trinity" and since the Lord's name sanctifies man the Christian thus receives his name in the Church. It can be the name of a saint, a faithful follower of Christ, or express a Christian mystery or virtue. The Catechism of the Catholic Church instructs us that the name one receives is a name for eternity.

Catechism of the Catholic Church: 405; 978; 977-980; 1212 - 16; 1257-1274; 2156 - 2159.
Bible: Jn 3:5: Mk 16:15-16; Rom 6:4; 4:25; 2 Pet 1:4; 1 Cor 6:19; 12:23; Mt 28:19-20; Rev 2:17; 14:1; Eph 4:25.

Questions to answer:

1. Name at least 2 times when angels played a role in announcing salvation to mankind.

2. How long have angels existed? Did God create angels or man and woman first?

3. Why was the sin of the angels irrevocable?

4. Why are the good holy angels in awe at the mercy of God?

•••

POINTS FOR PARENTS AND TEACHERS

This lesson, like all others in this book, aims to give young Catholics the opportunity to think about their holy religion which is "supernatural" and not merely "natural"

Catholics should realize the extent of God's love for mankind. "...God so loved the world that he gave his only-begotten Son, that those who believe in him may not perish, but may have life everlasting" (John 3:16).

From their earliest years, children should be taught to refer to the Trinity as "THREE PERSONS in ONE GOD" so they do not think of the Father, the Son and the Holy Spirit as being "three individual Gods."

Parents and teachers should emphasize that Jesus is the universal Savior— the Savior of all mankind. Often those who are not properly instructed erroneously conclude that Christians have one Savior while people of other religions have others.

Daily duty done as perfectly as possible in the spirit of penance is the sacrifice God expects from His people.

LESSON 4
MEN ARE PERSONS
MADE OF BODY AND SOUL

God is eternal. He had no beginning and will have no end. Man, however, was created by God and had a beginning. But man, like God, will have no end because his soul will live forever.

The Bible states that man was made in the image (likeness) of God. When God created man out of nothing, He gave him a body and soul. Man's body helps him understand a little about God's goodness and power, but his soul reflects much more the glory of the Creator.

The soul is a spirit which cannot be seen. Although it is invisible to human eyes, the soul is, nevertheless, real and immortal. (Immortal means it will live forever.) Indeed, it is difficult for men to understand the meaning of "forever." For even if one were to multiply all the grains of sand on earth by the greatest imaginable number, the product would still be a mere hint of how long "forever" really is.

Unlike his soul, man's body can be seen. It was born in time and someday will die and return to dust. However, in one sense, the body, too, will live forever; for at the end of the world, it will rise from the dead, be reunited to the soul and never again be subject to death. (This is what is meant by the resurrection of the dead.) If the soul is in heaven at this general resurrection, the body will share in its perfection and beauty.

*God gave man an immortal soul
which will live forever.*

On the contrary, if the soul is in hell, the body, upon being reunited to it, will become extremely ugly and horrible.

Animals, unlike men, do not have spiritual souls. Therefore, their life is completely ended when they die. Neither can animals know with a mind nor love with a will. Man is the only earthly creature who possesses an immortal soul and the great powers of knowing and loving. Since these gifts make man most like his Creator, they should be appreciated and used well.

Both man's body and soul are important because TOGETHER they make up the complete human person. When God became Man, He took a human body and soul. The Incarnation (God becoming Man) raised the dignity of man and also showed God's love for him. God never became an angel, but the Second Person of the Blessed Trinity did become a man. Although the Person of Jesus always was, His body and soul were created in time and made one with His Divine Person.

Man's life begins when God creates his body and soul, but it continues forever. How important it is that every person live his earthly life well! By doing so, he will save his soul which will one day be reunited to his body for all eternity in heaven.

REVIEW QUESTIONS

1. What is man?

Man is a creature made of body and soul, created by God in His own image and likeness.

2. How is the soul of man like God?

The soul of man is like God because it is a spirit. However, God is infinite or without limit in His spiritual being; whereas, man is limited. Man is, nevertheless, like God because his soul has understanding and free will and will live forever.

DISCUSSION QUESTIONS

1. Out of what did God make man?
2. What will happen to the soul after the body dies and returns to dust?
3. How long will the soul live?
4. How is man like God?
5. Will the body ever be reunited with the soul after death? Explain.
6. Does an animal live on in any way after its death? Explain.
7. Was the body and soul of Jesus created in time?
8. Was the Person of Jesus created in time?
9. To what earthly creature did God give the highest and most noble dignity?

●●●

FOR OLDER STUDENTS

In the fullness of time God kept His promise of a Redeemer which He made in Genesis 3:15 after Adam and Eve had fallen. God the Father sent His own divine Son, the Second Person of the Blessed Trinity, conceived and born with a human nature in the fullness of time of the Woman, Mary, who was overshadowed by the Holy Spirit. The Blessed Virgin Mary freely consented to become the Mother of the Son of the Most High, the Word made flesh. Mary represented the human race in speaking for all mankind in freely accepting its Savior. God never forces salvation upon anyone. Mary was free in accepting the vocation to become the Mother of God and finally Mother of the Church.

We have the power to believe that Jesus is the Son of God by the grace of the Holy Spirit. Jesus Christ, true God and true man, is at the very heart and center of all true catechesis.

It is all important for salvation to have a faith in and understanding of Who Jesus is and what He means. Jesus means "God Saves" and Christ means "Anointed One" or Messiah. Our faith must appreciate the meaning of St. John the Apostle when he says, "The Word became flesh." Mary remained "ever-virgin" in conceiving and giving birth to Jesus Christ. The Bible speaks of the "brothers and sisters" of Jesus but the Church has always taught that these passages refer not to other children of the Virgin Mary but to relatives or cousins of Jesus. The Catechism of the Catholic Church explains from the Bible itself why they could not be other children of Mary.

While the Person of Jesus as Son of God is infinite and equal to the Father, yet the Son, Who is the Word of God, took on a human body that is finite. The Church approves then of portraying the human face of Jesus and showing him in holy images. Jesus reveals to us in a human way the love of God the Father for us. To save all mankind from sin Jesus Christ suffered, was crucified on the Cross, died and was buried. Jesus after death descended into hell, or realms of the dead, prior to His Resurrection. The supreme proof that Jesus is God was His Resurrection. The empty tomb on the first Easter Sunday, and His many appearances to reliable witnesses after His Resurrection, bear testimony that Jesus Christ is true God, true Man, the Way, Truth and Life and Light of the world - the universal Savior for people of every nation.

Jesus ascended into heaven after having remained on earth after His Resurrection for 40 days. He is now seated at the right hand of God the Father, living there to make intercession for us. At the end of the world, on Judgment Day, Jesus will come again and judge each one. Then Jesus, the Redeemer of the world, will pass final judgment on the works and hearts of each one which will be brought to light for all.

Catechism of the Catholic Church: 422-451; 476- 507; 659-678.

Bible: Gal 4:4-5 Mk 1:1,11; Lk 1:55,68; Jn 13:3; 1 Jn 1:1—4; Phil 3:8-11; Mt. 1:21; 2:7; Rom 3:25; 10:6-13; 1 Cor 2:8 Jn 20:28; Jn 21:7; Heb 9:26: Lk 24:26-27,44-45; Acts 3:a5; Rom 8:11; 1 Cor 15:3-4; Jn 11:44; 20:5-7; 1 Cor 15:5; Mt 1:20; 13:55; 28:1; 27:56; Mk 16:19 Dan 7:14: Rom 14:9; 2 Pet 3:13; Rev. 19:1-9.

Questions to Answer:

1. When did God first give mankind a promise and what was that promise?

2. How can Mary be perpetually a virgin and the Virgin Mother of the Church when the Bible speaks of the brothers and sisters of Jesus?

3. Why is the freedom of Mary important in her role of acceptance to be the Mother of the Savior?

4. What above all bears testimony that Jesus Christ is Lord, God and Savior?

*Catholics should have a great love
and devotion to Jesus in the Holy
Eucharist and frequently receive Him
in Holy Communion.*

POINTS FOR PARENTS AND TEACHERS

The content of this book proceeds from simple to complex and is gradually developed and expanded. Therefore, concepts presented in each lesson should be mastered before a new lesson is begun. Ideally, lessons should be studied in the order they appear in this book.

Many present-day catechetical programs do not provide adequate instruction on the immortality of the soul or the beauty of a soul filled with grace. Teachers and parents should help Catholic youth understand and appreciate these truths.

Young children, too, should learn about the soul. They must realize that it is the spiritual part of man, created in the image and likeness of God and destined for eternal happiness. But Catholics must realize that man will achieve his ultimate destiny and reward ONLY if he is faithful to his Catholic Christian Faith.

Young people should be taught that the "good life" must be built on a strong supernatural foundation. The earth with its satisfactions and pleasures can never be the goal of authentic Christians. Likewise, the virtues of generosity, kindness, love, etc., must be supernaturalized and rooted in Christ if they are to be truly Catholic.

LESSON 5
PRAYER IS LISTENING
AND TALKING TO GOD

God made us to know, love and serve Him. We do this when we pray.

Prayer consists not only of speaking to God but also listening to Him. Because God is a Spirit and cannot be seen, it is sometimes difficult to pray. But God has given us signs of His presence everywhere which help us lift up our minds and hearts to Him. Therefore, we are praying when we simply look at the sky, clouds or stars and remember that God has made them.

Although everything in the world was created beautiful and good, God gave man the highest dignity of any of His earthly creatures. We are praying when we merely think or say: "Dear God, You did this because You love us. Thank You."

When we recall God's presence in the world around us, we are truly listening to Him. We are also listening to God when we kneel in faith before the tabernacle in a Catholic Church and think: "Jesus Christ continues to live in our midst and loves us. He is truly present in the Blessed Sacrament."

When we are attentive to a sermon or a Bible reading, we are likewise listening to God. When a parent, teacher or employer instructs or gives us orders, we can, in truth, listen to God's voice through theirs. Whenever we respond to any person, place, event or thing and tell God in our own words that

God has given us signs of His presence
everywhere to help us lift up
our minds and hearts to Him.

we love Him, thank Him, are sorry for having offended Him, or ask His special blessings, we are praying.

Prayer is easy if we have faith. In fact, prayer is in itself an act of faith, hope and love. We should often ask the Third Person of the Blessed Trinity, the Holy Spirit, for the great gift of prayer. He is always ready to help us pray if we but ask for His assistance.

Although we can pray anytime or anywhere, there are particular moments and places that are especially suitable for prayer. The House of God, the Church, is the best place to pray. That is where Catholics come together to worship God and to fulfill their obligation of participating in the greatest of all prayers, the Holy Sacrifice of the Mass, every Sunday and Holy Day of Obligation.

There are also special times during each day when we should lift up our minds and hearts to God; for example, when we rise, before and after meals and before going to bed. At these moments, it is good to say some of the Church's approved prayers (which we should memorize) because these are most powerful when prayed attentively with faith and love. The Bishops of the United States said Catholics should understand and frequently pray the following prayers: The Our Father, Hail Mary, Apostles' Creed, Act of Contrition, Rosary and Sign of the Cross.

Whenever we say any prayers we have memorized, we must concentrate and try to mean each word we pray. Then we will be doing what God desires—praying with our lips and heart (cf. Isaiah 29:13).

There are times when we do not feel like praying. Nevertheless, we must. With faith and love, we give God our prayer, knowing He will accept our intention and reward our efforts. Sometimes we think He does not hear us because we do not get an answer as soon as we want it. But God knows what is best and always answers our prayers.

Jesus Himself has told us we must pray if we wish to go to heaven. Since God is our good Father, Creator and Friend, we, His creatures and children, must make the effort and take the time to listen and speak to Him often. When we do this, we are knowing, loving and serving God in this world and preparing for the perfection of such worship in heaven.

REVIEW QUESTIONS

1. What is prayer?

Prayer is listening and talking to God. Through it, we lift up our minds and hearts to God and know, love and serve Him. It is necessary to pray if we wish to save our souls.

2. Why do we pray to God?

There are four reasons why we pray to God:
1. To adore Him.
2. To thank Him.
3. To ask His forgiveness.
4. To ask Him for graces and favors for ourselves and others.

3. How should we pray?

We should pray with our minds and hearts attentive to what we are saying or to what God is saying to us. When we say prayers we have memorized, we must try to think of the words we are praying and mean them. We should persevere in prayer and pray with faith and trust because God is good and will always hear and answer us.

DISCUSSION QUESTIONS

1. When can a person pray?
2. Where can a person pray?
3. Name some special places most fitting for prayer.
4. Name some special times of the day when good Catholic Christians should pray.
5. What approved prayers of the Church have you memorized? How often do you pray these?
6. Make up a short prayer to God using your own words. If you wish, you may share this with others.
7. Do people have to pray? Explain.
8. How often should a good Catholic pray? Explain.
9. Are our prayers pleasing to God if we are distracted when we pray? Explain.
10. Why should everyone pray?
11. Should a person pray to God only when he wants or needs something? Explain.
12. Name some special persons for whom we should pray.
13. Prayers of reparation make up to God in some way for

one's own sins and the sins of others. Name some other things people can do that will repair for sin.

●●●

FOR OLDER STUDENTS

The Bible tells us that it is the heart that prays. Prayer is not sincere or fruitful if one's heart is far from God. Heart means not the physical organ but our inner being, our hidden center. The human heart of each one is very personal and cannot be grasped by others. The heart is the place of decision, of truth, where we choose life and covenant with God.

Christian prayer is a covenant relationship with God. It is opening our heart in humility to let the Holy Spirit act in us. For one baptized in Christ prayer is a living relationship with God the Father, in, with and through His Son Jesus Christ in the unity of the Holy Spirit.

God is always calling each person to encounter Him in prayer. Abraham and Jacob of the Old Testament of the Bible are examples of persevering in faith and trust in God with lives of prayer. The prayers of Moses foreshadowed the intercessory power of prayer of Jesus Christ, the one essential Mediator for mankind.

God's people under the Old Covenant flourished as they focused on God's dwelling place seen in the Ark of the Covenant and the Temple, as guided by King David and the prophets. The 150 Psalms of David present the best example of prayer in the Old Testament, expressing personal prayer and those of the community of God's people. The Psalms remain an essential part of the prayer of the Church. We shall come to realize that while we can pray at all times and places, today, the Catholic Church where the Sacrifice of Jesus is perpetuated and His Real Presence is in the Tabernacle, is the special place of God's dwelling and for special prayer and adoration as God directed.

The priestly prayer of Jesus, found at length in John 17, is of special importance in teaching us the heart of Jesus relative to His Father and us. Jesus taught us how to pray in teaching us the Lord's Prayer. The Our Father should be prayed only from the heart, meaning what we say.

Mary, as the perfect Christian of faith, gave examples of her prayer-life. There was her Fiat whereby she accepted God's Will to be His Mother and bring us our Savior. "Let it be it done to me as you say." Her Magnificat, "My being magnifies the Lord...." is an offering of her entire being to God in faith and trust.

The Catechism of the Catholic Church presents the traditional four purposes of prayer: 1. Blessing and Adoration; 2. Petition; 3. Intercession 4. Thanksgiving. It adds a fifth purpose, Prayer of Praise, closely associated with prayer of Adoration, as it is entirely disinterested and raises the soul to give God glory.

Catechesis, whether of children, young people or adults, is not successful unless it leads to meditation on the Word of God, appreciation of the liturgical prayers of the Sacrifice of the Mass and the Sacraments. Catechesis must lead us to have a spirit of prayer in one's heart at all times.

Every prayer is answered by God when offered in faith. The main difficulty in praying is distraction. A distraction tells us what we are attached to and offers us the opportunity to turn back to God, giving Him our heart to be purified.

Catechism of the Catholic Church: 2558-2564; 2566-2589; 2623 - 2850.

Bible: Lk 18:9-14; Rom 6:5; 8:26; Jn 4:10; Jn 4:10; Eph 3:9, 13 Acts 17:27; Heb 10:5-7; 11;17; Rom 8:32: 1 Tim 2:5 1 Sam 3:9-10; 1:9-18. Ezra 9:6-15; Neh 1:4-11; Jn 2:1-12; Jn 17; Lk 1:38; 22:42; 46-55; Mt 5:23-24, 44-45; 6: 21,24; 9:23; 21:22; Mk 10:22.

Questions to answer:

1. How does the Catholic Church as a place of worship and the tabernacle with the Most Blessed Sacrament replace today the temple and ark of the covenant of the Old Testament?

2. We cannot pray sincerely except from the heart. Explain what is mean by "heart".

3. When is the only time we are successful in the study of the Catechism or our holy Catholic faith?

4. What is meant by prayer being a covenant relationship with God?

POINTS FOR PARENTS AND TEACHERS

Many parents and educators have not taught young people about the power of prayer or helped them form good habits of prayer. Perhaps this is why so many young Catholics have become careless and indifferent about attending Mass on Sundays, fre-

quenting the sacraments and obeying the Commandments of God and the Church.

Without prayer, faith quickly disappears. Therefore, children must understand what prayer is, why we must pray and how to pray.

It is not enough to teach only the prayer of petition. Youth must know about the prayer of adoration, thanksgiving and reparation. The prayer of reparation will especially help them become aware of sin and its gravity.

Parents and teachers should encourage the following practices:

- Offering reparation to the Sacred Heart of Jesus and the Immaculate Heart of Mary.
- Making visits to the Blessed Sacrament.
- Attending Holy Hours and Vigils.
- Praying the traditionally approved prayers of the Church, especially the Litanies of the Sacred Heart of Jesus, the Blessed Virgin Mary and the Saints.
- Making reparation for contemporary sins of sacrilege, omission, indifference, immodesty, abortion, failures to worship and keep holy the Lord's Day, etc.

In short, adults should do all they can to help young people develop a filial love for Christ and His Holy Mother and a deep, personal relationship with Them.

In Basic Teachings for Catholic Religious Education, the Bishops spoke clearly and emphatically about the importance of prayer. They said, "This teaching will take place through experiences of prayer, through the example of prayer and through learning common prayer." They went on to say that religious education, whether at home or in the classroom, should provide both instruction and experience so the learner can gradually be led to advance in prayer. The Bishops' instruction on prayer is both timely and urgent. Adults should heed their requests.

LESSON 6
GRACE MAKES US CHILDREN OF GOD

All men are born as children of their earthly mothers and fathers. Thus, they receive both human life and human nature from their natural parents. At Baptism, however, men receive a new life—divine life—which comes to them from their heavenly Father. Through this sacrament, they are reborn in grace and become children of God. That is why we do not merely "call" God our Father; He truly "is" our Father. St. John writes clearly and at length about this in the Bible (I John 3).

"Life" is a word that often occurs in Scripture. Jesus told us that grace is a sharing in His own divine life. We call this sharing "sanctifying grace" because it makes our souls holy and pleasing to God. It also makes us temples of the Holy Spirit and gives us the right to heaven. Sanctifying grace is so important that no one can go to heaven unless he possesses it in his soul at death.

To better understand how sanctifying grace enables us to rise above our "natural life" and share in God's divine life, we should think of it as a power. Grace gives men the power to know and love God as He knows and loves Himself.

Men must strive to grow in grace every day because their union with God and eternal happiness will be in proportion to the degree of divine life they possess at death. Although everyone in heaven will be perfectly happy, not everyone will be equally happy. This truth can be better understood by the following comparison:

Just as different size glasses can be perfectly full, so souls with different capacities can be perfectly happy in heaven. However, men can, so to speak, increase their capacity by growing in grace. By doing so, they become "larger vessels or glasses" which can contain, as it were, more divine life. Those who grow in grace will receive a greater reward in heaven and be able to give God more glory throughout eternity. Although the life of the Holy Trinity is infinite (without limit), man's sharing in God's life is limited. When a person is born into grace at Baptism, the three Persons in one God come to live in Him. However, as time goes on, he should enter into a closer union with the Most Holy Trinity by growing in God's life or power.

Good works done for the love of God, prayer, sacrifice, attendance at Holy Mass and worthy reception of the sacraments (particularly the Holy Eucharist) are excellent means of growing in grace.

God has given images to some of His specially chosen children which help us better understand grace. For instance, He permitted St. Catherine of Siena to see a soul in sanctifying grace. Because its brightness and light were so beautifully overwhelming, this saint at first thought she was seeing God Himself! She said, "If I did not know there was only one God, I would have thought that this was another."

Indeed, the beauty and worth of a soul in the state of grace is beyond human understanding. It has correctly been said that one soul in grace is of greater value to God than the whole created universe. Men should, therefore, appreciate this gift of divine life and do all they can to preserve and increase it both in themselves and in others.

*Just as different size glasses
can be perfectly full, so souls with
different capacities can be
perfectly happy in heaven.*

REVIEW QUESTIONS

1. What is sanctifying grace?

Sanctifying grace is a sharing in the life of God Himself within the soul. It is a supernatural life which gives the soul the power to know and love God and to be happy with Him forever in heaven.

2. What are the chief effects of sanctifying grace?

A person in the state of sanctifying grace:
    1. Is holy and pleasing to God.
    2. Is an adopted child of God.
    3. Is a temple of the Holy Spirit.
    4. Has the right to heaven.

3. Can a soul grow in sanctifying grace?

Yes, a soul can and should grow in sanctifying grace every day of its life. It can do so by the following means:
    1. Prayer.
    2. The sacraments, especially the Holy Eucharist.
    3. The Holy Sacrifice of the Mass.
    4. Ordinary actions and daily duties performed in love for God.

DISCUSSION QUESTIONS

1. Using your own words, explain sanctifying grace.

2. Why are we truly God's children by adoption and not merely His children in name only?

3. Will everyone be equally happy in heaven? Explain.

4. How can we grow in sanctifying grace?

5. Explain why sanctifying grace is sometimes called "God-power. "

6. Can a person grow in sanctifying grace each day of his life? Explain.

●●●

FOR OLDER STUDENTS

It is through the power of the Holy Spirit that we receive grace to be justified. Justification means to be cleansed from sins so as to be given "the righteousness of God through faith in Jesus Christ". It come with Baptism.

The life of sanctifying grace begins with Baptism. The Holy Spirit then empowers us to take part in the Passion of Jesus Christ by being converted away from sin, and to share in Jesus' Resurrection by being born to a new life in Christ. We are then made members of Christ's Body which is the Church, like branches grafted onto Christ who is the Vine.

Justification or righteousness means that the theological virtues of faith, hope and charity, are poured into our hearts. We then desire to be obedient to God's will. These virtues are powers from God. This new life in Jesus Christ is sometimes called being in the state of sanctifying grace. Justification then comes from the free gift of God we call grace which makes us children of God, partakers of the divine nature and in possession of eternal life. This gift is free, for it was merited for us by Jesus Christ. Grace brings us into intimacy with the life of the Blessed Trinity.

Sanctifying grace is an habitual gift, for it remains stable in us so long as we do not commit mortal sin and we continue in faith and the love of God. It makes our souls pleasing in God's sight.

Actual grace is not constant in its action on the soul. It is fleeting, comes and goes. Actual grace comes from God, too. God intervenes with individual men to begin the process of conversion if one lacks faith or if one with faith is in mortal sin. Souls in grace are often, through actual grace, inspired to deeper union with God by the Holy Spirit stirring them to respond by drawing them to Himself. God can invite men to convert or come into deeper union with Him by things that occur in the ordinary course of the day. It may be the word of a friend; a sermon, a spiritual reading; the beauty of nature that reminds us of God. No one can merit the initial grace of conversion. We must first be moved by the Holy Spirit. Each one of the seven sacraments gives a special kind of grace to those properly disposed.

There are many special kinds of grace besides sanctifying and actual grace. There are special gifts oriented to sanctifying grace. There is the grace of a certain vocation or state in life. There is the grace of charisms, which according to St. Paul is a favor or gratuitous gift, a benefit for others. Such special gifts are for the service in charity of building up the Church.

It is important to distinguish the spirits so that one who

reportedly has special charisms is in fact leading souls to union in Jesus Christ, in peace and unity and is not of another spirit.

Catechism of the Catholic Church: 1987- 2016
Bible: Rom 3:21-26; 6:8-11; 12:6-8; Jn 1:12-18; Rom 8:14-17; 12:6-8; 2 Pet 1:3-4.

Questions to answer:

1. What does it mean to be justified and how does justification come?
2. Why is sanctifying grace also called "habitual" grace?
3. Can one really save his own soul or merit salvation?
4. Why can one in mortal sin never be restored to sanctifying grace unless he first responds to actual grace?

POINTS FOR PARENTS AND TEACHERS

It is important that young Catholics obtain a fundamental understanding of sanctifying grace. Without this knowledge, they cannot understand our life in Christ, the nature of the Church as the Mystical Body of Christ and other concepts that will be developed in subsequent lessons of this book.

Young people should know that our life in Christ (which consists of being in the state of grace) is not a static existence. It must continue to increase each day of our lives. The Mass, sacraments, daily prayers and good works are excellent ways to grow in the life of the Blessed Trinity.

Parents and teachers should also stress the following points:

- *Catholic Christians must strive to live a life that is super-naturally (and not merely naturally) good.*

- *Natural feelings do not necessarily indicate that one is in or advancing in grace; rather, an honestly and correctly formed conscience is the best guide for determining this.*

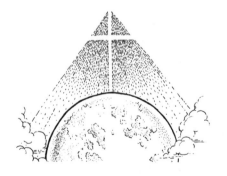

"I am the Vine; you are the branches. . ." **John 15:5**

Jesus Christ, the God-Man, founded only one Church, the Catholic Church. He told us this Church would be a living body and compared it to a plant, saying, "I am the vine, you are the branches...." (John 15:5).

When we understand grace as a sharing in God's life, we can better realize how men can be one in Christ's Mystical Body, the Church. Jesus is the invisible Head of the Church; the Holy Spirit, its Soul; and we, the People of God, its members.

The Church began with the death and resurrection of Christ. However, hundreds of years before Jesus came as our Savior, God the Father sent the prophets who prepared for Christ's mission of founding the Church. (The Old Testament of the Bible tells us about this.)

Only one Church, the Catholic Church, has the FULL deposit of truth. It has had the true faith and true sacraments as well as the powers Jesus gave to His first priests and bishops, the Apostles.

The Church, therefore, is not a building, an institution, or a natural organization; rather, it is the living Mystical Body of Christ in which the members meet, embrace and love the very Person of Jesus and each other.

The concept of the Mystical Body can be understood in

many ways. Jesus Himself likened the Church to a tree in which He was the trunk or vine and we, its branches (John 15:5). The sap in both vine and branches is the same—grace or the life of God. That is, the divine life in Jesus' soul is the very same life of God that fills every soul in the state of sanctifying grace.

Sometimes children find it helpful to compare the Mystical Body to the human body. As our physical bodies are made up of millions of living cells, so the Church is composed of millions of people who together make up one complete Body of Christ.

No matter what means is used to describe Christ's Church, it is necessary that one important fact be grasped. The Church consists of millions of people united in ONE faith and ONE Jesus who share ONE same baptism which makes them all ONE Church—ONE Mystical Body of Christ.

The Church is, therefore, truly a community, the People of God, with Jesus as its Leader and Head. The Holy Spirit, Who dwells in each member of this body, makes them all holy and keeps the Church united in one true faith.

When some people say, "I will accept Jesus but not the Church," they do not realize what the Church really is. In the Bible, Our Lord Himself said that he who rejects the Church, rejects Christ (Matt. 18:17 cf). Furthermore, men cannot be saved unless they accept and belong to the Church because Jesus has established this Divine Organism as the instrument by which He wishes to save all men. By being members of the Church, we are, in truth, members of God's own family.

REVIEW QUESTIONS

1. What is the Church?

The Church is the People of God who have been baptized into Christ Jesus and share the one same true faith that is from God. The Church is a community, God's Family, who together share the life of Christ. With the Pope as the world's chief Bishop and the other Catholic bishops in union with him, God's People are kept in the one true faith through the power of the Holy Spirit. In this Church, which is also called the Mystical Body of Christ, we have the Mass and sacraments which give glory to God and grace to souls.

2. Why is the Church called "the Mystical Body of Christ"?

The Church is called "the Mystical Body of Christ" in order to distinguish it from His physical body. But as the human body has many different members (feet, hands, eyes, ears, nose, heart, etc.) all joined together to form ONE complete body, so the Church has many members joined together as ONE in the Body of Christ by their baptism and profession of the true faith.

DISCUSSION QUESTIONS

1. What is the name of the supernatural life in our souls which makes us live "in Christ"?

2. Who is the invisible Head of the Church? Why is He called the "invisible" Head?

3. Who is the Soul of the Church?

4. Who are the members of the Church?

5. Does the Catholic Church have all or only some part of the true faith? Explain.

6. Explain the following statement: The Church is not merely an institution; rather, it is Jesus Christ living in the world today.

7. How does Jesus' example of the vine and branches help us understand the Church as Christ's Mystical Body?

8. Explain how the rejection of the Church is a rejection of Jesus Christ.

●●●

FOR OLDER STUDENTS

The word "Church" is a from a Greek word "ek-ka-lein," which means to "call out of" or calling together of an assembly of people for a religious purpose. In the Old Testament God called His Chosen People together at Mount Sinai where, through Moses, they were given the Ten Commandments. At that time they were made God's holy people.

When the first Christian believers called themselves "Church" it was to recognize that they were heirs to that first assembly God formed of people in the Old Testament times. In the Church today, which lives under the New Covenant, God is calling together His people from the entire world into one fold, in one faith, under one shepherd.

The "Church" today means a liturgical assembly. The local church is when people come together to celebrate the Holy Eucharist. Jesus becomes present in the midst of His people then, perpetuating His Sacrifice of the Cross.Jesus then also offers Himself in Holy Communion to strengthen His union with His people. In this way all the baptized members of the Church become stronger in their union with Jesus and each other as the Body of Christ by growing in grace which is their participation in the divine nature.

The Church as the "Mystical Body of Christ" is but one expression of the reality of the Church as used by St. Paul in the Bible. Jesus Himself spoke of the Vine and Branches to teach His union with members of the Church. The Church is also spoken of in the Bible as a sheepfold, a cultivated field, the building of God like many bricks bond together into one building. The Church is the Bride of Christ and the Temple of the Holy Spirit.

The Church is both human and divine. It is both visible and spiritual. It has a hierarchical society with Pope, bishops, deacons, priests and baptized members with various states of life. The Bishop is the head of the local Church and the Pope is head of the universal Church. The Bishop is also subject to the Pope. Priests, and all the faithful, are subject to their bishops.

The Church bears divine life of grace to us and only through the Church can we render the infinitely pleasing worship which God desires from mankind in, with and through Jesus Christ. The Church will receive its perfection only in the glory of heaven. Yet the Church gives men grace and forgiveness of sin while it gives, even now, infinitely pleasing worship to God the Father through Jesus Christ in the unity of the Holy Spirit who is the Sanctifier and Soul of the Church.

The four characteristics or marks of the true Church are: One, Holy, Catholic, and Apostolic. All four must be present for the fullness of revealed truth and divine powers which Jesus gave to His one Church.

Oneness of the Church is seen in one Lord, one faith, one baptism, forming only one Body of Christ. Loyal Catholics remain in union with the true Church of Jesus Christ by believing the same doctrines of faith and morals throughout the world.

The Church is Holy because She was founded by Jesus Christ the Head. This Church through its teachings and Sacraments has the power to make her members holy and to forgive their sins. She is holy in her saints. Mary, Mother of the Church, is already all-holy. She is therefore the Model of what the Church is and hopes to become.

The true Church is Catholic, meaning she proclaims the

fullness of true faith for men of all nations with the same doctrines and authority of Christ everywhere. Since there is a
unity of the human race under one God there must be but one
Church that is universal or Catholic.

The true Church is Apostolic meaning the Church which
Jesus Christ founded was built on the twelve apostles. The true
Church is indestructible. The Catholic Church will be here
until the end of the world and it alone has the fullness of
divinely revealed truth reaching back to the days of Jesus
Christ and the first twelve Apostles on earth.

The Second Vatican Council (*Lumen Gentium* 8) was
quoted by the universal Catechism of the Catholic Church in
saying: "The sole Church of Christ which in the Creed we
profess to be one, holy, catholic, and apostolic, ... subsists in
the Catholic Church, which is governed by the successor of
Peter and by the bishops in communion with him.
Nevertheless, many elements of sanctification and of truth are
found outside its visible confines."

The same document of the sacred synod of Vatican
Council II, also quoted by the universal Catechism said the
following of the Catholic Church: "Basing itself upon sacred
Scripture and Tradition, the Council teaches that the Church,
a pilgrim now on earth, is necessary for salvation: the one
Christ is the mediator and the way of salvation; he is present to
us in his body which is the Church. He himself explicitly
asserted the necessity of faith and Baptism, and thereby
affirmed at the same time the necessity of the Church which
men enter through Baptism as through a door. Hence they
could not be saved who, knowing that the Catholic Church
was founded as necessary by God through Christ, would refuse
either to enter it or to remain in it." (Lumen Gentium 14)

Jesus Christ instituted the Church with the Apostles as first bishops forming a college or permanent assembly at the head of which Jesus placed Peter, chosen from among them. The Pope by divine institution possesses supreme, full, immediate, and universal power in the care of souls.

The inspired Word of God in sacred scripture tells us that the Church is the "Pillar and bulwark of the truth". It "has received this solemn command of Christ from the apostles to announce the saving truth" (1 Tim 3:15). The Church has been given the sacred "deposit" of faith and morals as teachings from God through the power of the Holy Spirit, the Spirit of truth. This Holy Spirit works in the Church through the Magisterium to keep the teachings of the Church in the truth.

St. John in his Gospel speaks repeatedly of the Spirit of truth which would be given to the Church to keep the Church in the truth taught by Jesus Christ who is the Truth (Jn 14:17; 15:26; 16;13). St. Luke's Gospel quotes Jesus saying: "He who hears you, hears me; and he who rejects you, rejects me; and he who rejects me, rejects him who sent me" (Lk 10:16).

Catechism of the Catholic Church: 748 - 975
Bible: Acts 1:8; 9:13; 19:39; Acts 10:35; 1 Cor 4:1; 9:1; 15:7-8; 11:18; 3:9; 13; 6:1; 16:1; 2 Cor 3:6; 6:4; 5:20; Eph 1:22-23; 2:20; 4:3; Jn 1:16-20; 3:13-19; Rev. 21:14 Mt 13:1-17; Mk. 16:16; Jn 35; Col 1:18; 3:14; Gal 4:19; Jn 1:4; 21:15-17; Mt 16:18-19; Mt. 10:40; 28:16-20.

Questions to answer:

1. What is the meaning of "Church"?

2. Name at least four expressions in the Bible used to speak of the Church.

3. Why must all four characteristics of the true Church be present for it to be the true Church of Jesus Christ in its fullness?

4. Why must the true Church have a successor to St. Peter?

5. Why does the expression of the Bible that the Church is the "Pillar and bulwark of the truth" demonstrate that God intended our faith to remain secure and in truth by listening to the voice of Jesus Christ in and through His Church and not simply by our private interpretation of the Bible?

POINTS FOR PARENTS AND TEACHERS

In Basic Teachings for Catholic Religious Education, *which was approved by the Vatican, our Bishops said: "In the Catholic Church are found the deposit of faith, the sacraments, and the ministries inherited from the apostles. Through these gifts of God, the Church is able to act and grow as a community in Christ, serving mankind and giving men his saving word and activity.... The Church is a community sharing together the life of Christ, a people assembled by God....In each (rite, diocese, parish, and mission), no matter how small or poor or isolated, 'Christ is present, and by his power, the one, holy, Catholic and Apostolic Church is gathered together.'"*

In this lesson, young people should realize that the Catholic Church is not merely an establishment or natural organization; instead, it is a Divine Organism, a living Body of Christ, and Jesus in His people. Therefore, the powers, the teachings and the activity of the Church are essentially those of Christ Jesus, Our Lord and Savior.

If youth were taught and understood by faith the supernatural reality of the Church as a community of the faithful which forms the Mystical Body of Christ, there would not be an identity crisis within the Church or young people who say they believe in God and accept Jesus but not the Church. Both situations indicate a need to understand Jesus' purpose in coming to earth and His clear identification with the Church—which, according to His promise, will never be destroyed.

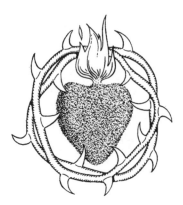

"In front...of Our Lady's right hand was a heart encircled with thorns which pierced it. . . this was the Immaculate Heart of Mary, outraged by the sins of *humanity...." —Sister Lucia of Fatima

LESSON 8
THE POPE IS THE VISIBLE HEAD OF THE CHURCH

Jesus is the "invisible" Head of the Church; the Pope is its "visible" head. We cannot see Christ with our human eyes but we can see the Vicar of Christ, our Holy Father, the Pope. His picture often appears in newspapers and magazines, and we can even watch him on television from time to time. The Pope lives in Rome, Italy, at "Vatican City."

Jesus continuously guides His Church from heaven and always remains its "invisible" Head. Such is not the case with the mortal, visible head of Christ's Mystical Body. When a Pope dies, it is necessary for the Cardinals to meet and elect a new Sovereign Pontiff. It was Our Lord Himself Who gave special power in His Church to St. Peter by making him the chief teacher and ruler of the entire Church (Matt. 16:18-19). Christ intended that the power given to St. Peter should be passed down to his successor, the Pope. As a result, the Catholic Church has always had a Pope, and the line of succession has remained unbroken down through the centuries. To date, there have been 262 Popes in all.

There is only one person on earth who possesses supreme power in Jesus' Name—the Vicar of Christ. Therefore, he is not simply a president or person holding a high place of honor; he is truly the visible head of Christ's Church. This truth is clearly expressed in Holy Scripture and has been reaffirmed by the traditional teachings of the Church as well as

The Holy Father, the Pope, is the direct
successor of St. Peter, whom Jesus made
the first Pope of the Catholic Church.
The Vicar of Christ is the only person
on earth who possesses supreme power in
Jesus' Name. Catholics owe him
undivided loyalty.

Catholic practices which date back to the first century.

Actually, the Holy Father is a bishop—but a very special one because he alone has supreme spiritual authority over all the baptized. (This includes other bishops, priests, religious and laity.) When all the other bishops of the world are united, they are called the "College of Bishops." The Pope, as the first or highest bishop, is the head of the College of Bishops who remain united with and under him.

The Pope is infallible, or cannot make a mistake, when all the following conditions are observed in any of his teachings:

1. He speaks on faith and morals.
2. He addresses himself to the entire or universal Church and not a mere part of it.
3. He indicates that he is speaking as the supreme teacher on faith and morals and that all Catholics must accept his teaching.

A Pope can teach infallibly (without error) for Jesus Christ in two ways:

1. Alone, which is referred to as "from the Chair of Peter," or
2. Together with the "College of Bishops."

It is important that all Catholics realize the Pope can speak infallibly by himself, but the College of Bishops can never speak infallibly without the Pope.

Catholics believe that the Third Person of the Blessed Trinity is speaking when the Pope teaches infallibly because Christ said the Holy Spirit would keep His Church true in its teachings and free from all error. Jesus Himself called the Holy Spirit the "Spirit of Truth," and this Spirit protects the Church through the Pope and College of Bishops in union with him, especially in Ecumenical Council (John 14:16-17 and John 15:26).

Whenever the Pope speaks on subjects like the Holy Eucharist, the Blessed Virgin Mary, prayer, how to live a life of purity, etc., all Catholics must accept what he says in preference to any other person's teachings or viewpoints. It is certain that they are listening to and obeying God when they listen to and obey Christ's Vicar on earth. Catholics should also follow and accept the Pope's daily teachings for he often uses these to reaffirm or apply the true faith to a specific issue, need or circumstance.

The People of God owe the Holy Father their filial love, respect, loyalty and prayers. The Pope's responsibilities and powers are great because they come directly from God, Eternal Truth, Who has said: "...thou art Peter, and upon this rock I will build my Church, and the gates of hell shall not prevail against it. And I will give thee the keys of the kingdom of heaven; and whatever thou shalt bind on earth shall be bound in heaven, and whatever thou shalt loose on earth shall be loosed in heaven" (Matt. 16:18-19).

*The Pope is the visible head of the holy
Catholic Church and the successor of
St. Peter, the Apostle. He lives in
the Vatican in Rome.*

REVIEW QUESTIONS

1. Who is the invisible Head of the Catholic Church?

Jesus Christ is the continuous invisible Head of the Catholic Church.

2. Who is the visible head of the Catholic Church?

The Pope is the visible head of the Catholic Church. He is the successor of St. Peter the Apostle and lives in the Vatican at Rome.

3. What does "infallibility of the Church" mean?

Infallibility of the Church is that quality by which the Church is kept free from error (mistakes) in matters of faith and morals by the Holy Spirit. Infallibility does not mean the Church gives its members new revelations; rather, it means the Church correctly interprets the deposit of faith given it by Jesus Christ.

4. Did Jesus promise infallibility of interpretation to anyone other than the Pope?

No, Jesus did not promise infallibility of interpretation to any individual or group of individuals except the Pope and the College of Bishops united with and under the Pope as its chief head. Vatican Council II restated this teaching of the Church. Therefore, it is false to say that since we are the Church, the Holy Spirit guides us equally.

5. When does the Catholic Church teach infallibly?

The Catholic Church teaches infallibly when it defines a doctrine of faith or morals which must be held by all the faithful. The Pope may define such a doctrine alone or the Church may define a doctrine of faith or morals through the College of Bishops speaking in union with the Holy Father.

DISCUSSION QUESTIONS

1. What does papal infallibility mean?
2. What three conditions must be present when the Pope teaches infallibly?
3. Could all the bishops of the world speak infallibly without the Pope? Explain.
4. Does the Holy Spirit guide all persons equally so each can understand faith and Christian morals infallibly? Explain.
5. Should we accept and follow the Pope's teachings only when he speaks infallibly?

●●●

FOR OLDER STUDENTS

The Church as instituted by Jesus Christ has a hierarchical constitution. This means Jesus established His Church with mission and authority especially invested in the Pope and bishops. Without this hierarchy of Pope and bishops, bodies which call themselves "Christian" are an imitation but not the full reality of the true Church instituted by Jesus Christ and promised to endure. Only to the one Church which He instituted and promised would last until the end of the world did Jesus give divine powers and infallible teachings with the Holy Spirit as its Soul to keep members of the Church in true faith.

When Jesus Christ instituted the Twelve Apostles He constituted them to form a college or permanent assembly, at the head of which he placed Peter, chosen from among the Twelve. Only Peter was made the "Rock" of Christ's Church and was given the keys of Christ's Church. The papacy is the Rock to keep the Church in true faith. The role given Peter by Jesus is not merely symbolic or an example for us of Peter's strong faith. The papacy is the reality Jesus promised to keep the Church in the truth always as guided by the Holy Spirit. Jesus Christ thus instituted Peter as the first pope or shepherd of the whole flock of the universal Church.

The Pope is the Bishop of the Diocese of Rome, the place where he lives. Vatican City is a separate State surrounded by the City of Rome and houses the administrative responsibilities of the universal Church with the Pope as visible head. The Pope is the chief shepherd of all dioceses of the world. He is known as the Roman Pontiff. Even bishops are subject to the Pope.

The Pope as pastor of the universal Church has full, supreme, and universal power of authority over the Church throughout the world. This power of authority given him by Jesus Christ can always be exercised unhindered. He does not depend on the bishops to exercise his full authority; they rather depend on him, ultimately upon Jesus Christ and the active protection of the Holy Spirit.

The college of bishops scattered throughout the world has no authority to act as a group or college unless they are unified with the Roman Pontiff, the successor of St. Peter. The college of bishops, as successors to the Apostles, also has "supreme and full authority over the universal Church," says the Catechism of the Catholic Church, echoing the teaching of the Second Vatican Council, while adding, "but this power cannot be exercised without the agreement of the Roman Pontiff" (*Lumen Gentium* 22).

The Pope and bishops of the universal Church are known as the Magisterium of the Church. What is the mission of the Magisterium? Through the assistance of the Holy Spirit the Magisterium guarantees the faithful that when they accept the teachings of the Church on faith and morals they can know and objectively profess the fullness of true faith without error. The members of the Church are thus able to live in the truth that makes them free.

The shepherds of the Church, working in union with the successor of St. Peter, thus have the charism of infallibility in matters of faith and morals. This is true especially when gathered in an Ecumenical Council of the Church, when such a Council makes final decisions of faith or morals for the entire Church and such is promulgated by the Holy Father, the Pope.

The Roman Pontiff, head of the college of bishops, may exercise infallibility alone or collectively with the college of bishops.

The Dogmatic Constitution on the Church states: "The sole Church of Christ [is that] which our Savior, after his Resurrection, entrusted to Peter's pastoral care, commissioning him and the other apostles to extend and rule it" (*Lumen Gentium* 8 p2).

Catechism of the Catholic Church: 874- 892.

Bible: Mt 16:18-19; Jn 17:21-23; Jn 21:15-17; Mk 16:15; Rom 10; 14-17.

Questions to answer:

1. What is meant by the hierarchical constitution of the Church and did Jesus found His Church in this way?

2. How does the authority of Pope differ from the authority of the other bishops of the Church?

3. What is the Magisterium of the Church?

4. Can a true Church exist without such a Magisterium? Give reason for answer.

5. What is meant by infallibility of the Church?

●●●

POINTS FOR PARENTS AND TEACHERS

Parents and educators must teach young people that Christ built His Church on the Rock of the Papacy and that Catholics should show great respect and loyalty to our Holy Father, the Pope.

Unfortunately, some people today are not following the teachings of the Church on papal authority. Vatican II clearly reconfirms the Church's position in this matter. Parents and teachers should carefully read and study the Dogmatic Constitution on the Church, Lumen Gentium, *in order to understand the special power given to the Pope as chief teacher and ruler of the entire Church.*

In regard to the erroneous thinking that Catholics must accept and follow the Pope's teaching ONLY when he solemnly defines doctrine, Lumen Gentium *states: "This religious submission of will and of mind must be shown in a special way to the authentic teaching of the Roman Pontiff even when he is not speaking ex* cathedra. That is, it must be shown in such a way that his supreme magisterium is acknowledged with reverence, the judgments made by him are sincerely adhered to, according to his manifest mind and will. His mind and will in the matter may be known chiefly either from the character of the documents, from his frequent repetition of the same doctrine, or from his manner of speaking."

●●●

LESSON 9
MARY IS THE MOTHER
OF THE CHURCH

Mary is the Mother of Jesus Christ, the God-Man. Therefore, the Church has rightly called her the Mother of God and Mother of all men.

Christ's Mystical Body, the Church, is united as a family with its Head, Jesus. Mary, Mother of the Head, is also Mother of the members.

Catholics must love and honor their spiritual mother, the Blessed Virgin Mary, if they wish to be sincere and true members of Christ's Church. Mary, who always leads people to her Divine Son, was blessed by God more than all the angels and saints put together. God loved her so much that He chose her to be His very own Mother. Mary, acting freely, agreed to do God's will and became Mother of the Savior and Mother of the Church at one and the same time.

We can learn much about Mary, the perfect Christian and great woman of faith, from the Bible. Her simple, holy life was filled with both sorrows and joys. She lived in Nazareth with Jesus and St. Joseph and faithfully did her daily duties and chores. She was always ready to help others and once made a long trip to assist her cousin, Elizabeth. Mary prayed constantly; in fact, she made everything she did a prayer.

Mary had many sufferings during her life. She felt sadness and grief at the death of her good husband, St. Joseph. As

Mary is the Mother of Jesus Christ,
the God-Man, and Mother of the Church.

Mary stood at the foot of the Cross and watched Jesus die, she felt the pain of men's sins as a sword piercing her own Immaculate Heart. The Holy Mother of God alone understood how much sin wounded the Sacred Heart of her Divine Son. By being humble, faithful and obedient, Mary proved her love in all that she did and was and became great in the sight of God and men.

St. Joseph was Mary's true husband and the VIRGINAL father of Jesus. He cared for Our Lord and took the place of Jesus' real eternal Father, the First Person of the Blessed Trinity. Mary's role was different. She was truly Jesus' real physical mother as she is our real spiritual mother. Our Lord could rightly speak of God the Father as "...my Father and your Father..." (John 20:17). He could also speak of Mary as "my Mother and your Mother." In fact, that is precisely how He presented Mary to us through His beloved disciple, St. John, when He said from the Cross, "...Woman, behold, thy son....Behold, thy mother...." (John 19:26-27).

Mary had only ONE Child and that Child was Jesus. Thus, she was and remains the ever-virgin Mother of Our Lord and Savior. After her Divine Son, Mary enjoys the highest place in the Church because she did God's will perfectly and never committed the slightest sin. She was even exempt from original sin, which all the other children of Adam inherit. When she died, Mary's body and soul were taken to heaven. (This is what is meant by the Assumption of the Blessed Virgin Mary.) From her beautiful throne, the Mother of God continues to love and pray for all her children still living on earth.

When we pray to Mary, we are really asking her to pray to God for us. When we love and honor Mary, we are imitating her Divine Son, Whose love and respect for her can never be equalled.

Recently, the Bishops of the United States listed the following prayers, which they said Catholics should understand, memorize and frequently pray: The Our Father, Hail Mary, Apostles' Creed, Act of Contrition, Rosary and Sign of the Cross. Notice that most of these prayers are contained in the Rosary which Our Lady of Fatima asked us to pray each day.

When both our bishops and Christ's Mother direct us (as they have) to pray, we dare not be indifferent to their instructions. By obeying them, we will certainly give honor to God and do His will.

REVIEW QUESTIONS

1. Is Mary truly the Mother of God?

Yes, it is a doctrine of Catholic Faith that Mary is truly God's Mother. In their Pastoral Letter, "Behold Your Mother," the Bishops of the United States said, "In the liturgy, 'we honor Mary the ever-virgin Mother of Jesus Christ our Lord and God' (Eucharistic Prayer D; 'Mary, the virgin Mother of God' (Prayers II and III); and 'the Virgin Mary, the Mother of God' (Prayer IV)."

2. Was Mary "ever-a-virgin"?

Yes, Mary was "ever-a-virgin." This means that Mary was a virgin before Jesus was born and remained a virgin during and after the birth of her Divine Son. Our Bishops in their Marian Pastoral Letter, "Behold Your Mother," said: "Catholic belief in the Virgin birth rests not on the Scriptures alone, but on the constant and consistent faith of the Church. Faith on this precise point has been expressed in many ways from the time of St. Matthew and St. Luke to the present."

3. Did Mary have other children?

No, Mary did not have any children other than Jesus. Mary was the real physical mother of Jesus, and Joseph was His virginal foster father. This truth of our Catholic Faith was reconfirmed by the Bishops of the United States in their Marian Letter, "Behold Your Mother," when they stated:

"The truth that Mary remained always a virgin, that is, that she had no other children...emerges clearly in the Church's consciousness in the fourth century, when 'ever- virgin' became a common description of her...St. Jerome faced the difficulties in such Biblical expressions as 'brothers of the Lord.' He showed that in New Testament Greek this term can mean 'cousins' as well as 'blood brothers.' "

4. Is Mary the Mother of the Church?

Yes, Mary is the Mother of the Church. This beautiful title was announced by Pope Paul VI during Vatican Council II and refers to the spiritual Motherhood of Mary. Mary, Mother of Jesus, is both Mother of the Head and Mother of the members of the Mystical Body, the Church.

5. Who is the Patroness of the United States?

Mary, the Mother of God, under the title of the Immaculate Conception was chosen Patroness of the United States by our bishops on May 13, 1846.

DISCUSSION QUESTIONS

1. Why is Mary called the "Woman of Faith"?
2. Name some of the great sufferings Mary had to endure during her life on earth.
3. Why is the title "Mother of the Church" so fitting for Mary?
4. What does "Mary, ever-virgin" mean?
5. Why must we honor and love Mary?
6. What are we really doing when we pray to Mary?
7. Was St. Joseph Jesus' real father? Explain.
8. Was St. Joseph Mary's real husband? Explain.
9. Was Mary Jesus' real mother? Explain.
10. Was Mary's soul ever stained by sin? Explain.

●●●

FOR OLDER STUDENTS

Mary is both Mother of the Head of the Church, Jesus Christ, and Mother of the members of the Mystical Body of Christ, the Church. Mary's role is inseparable from her union with Jesus Christ as His Mother. The inseparability of the Hearts of Jesus and Mary are manifest in the Bible from the moment of Christ's virginal conception until His death.

Mary is the eschatological Icon of the Church. In Mary we can see what the Church already is in her mystery in this pilgrimage of faith" and what the Church will become in heaven at the end of this journey. Only in the Head of the Church while on earth and in the Mother of the Church on earth was there perfection in every respect.

After Jesus ascended into heaven Mary helped the beginnings of the Church by her example and prayers. She is known as the "Queen of the Apostles", "Queen of the Clergy" and "Help of Christians" among many other titles. It was Mary who gathered with the disciples in the upper room, (cenacle) after Jesus ascended into heaven, imploring with them the gift of the Holy Spirit upon the Church. Mary had been overshadowed by the Holy Spirit at the annunciation and conception of Jesus and would now have the Holy Spirit descend upon her in a special way on Pentecost Sunday, known as the birthday of the Church.

The Second Vatican Council issued the most extensive document ever issued on Mary in its 8th chapter of the Dogmatic Constitution of the Church, (Lumen Gentium). The Fathers of this Council taught of Mary together with their pronouncements on the Church to indicate a balance in Church teachings on the Mother of God. Just as Jesus and Mary are inseparable, so Mary must not be separated from the Church in teaching her role in the economy of salvation. There is a Marian dimension to the Church. Mary is our Mother in the order of grace.

Mary, having been assumed body and soul into heaven, has

not laid aside her saving role of consent and intercession. She continues to intercede that we accept the gifts of eternal salvation from Jesus Christ, the Source and one essential Mediator. The second Vatican Council said that the Church invokes Mary under "the titles of Advocate, Helper, Benefactress, and Mediatrix."

By hearing the word of God and keeping it perfect in her Heart, the Blessed Virgin Mary shared in Christ's sufferings and rejection. She cooperated in His saving work. She spiritually followed her Son as she had done during His hidden life in Nazareth.

Mary's intervention at the wedding feast of Cana is most instructive on the powerful role of Mary's intercession with the Sacred Heart of her divine Son. As the Woman of faith Mary was instrumental in this first miracle of Jesus changing water into vine in leading the Apostles to have faith in Jesus Christ. The Apostle John ends the Cana account of his Gospel with: "Thus did he reveal his glory, and his disciples believed in him."

The Second Vatican Council emphasized Mary's participation in the public life of Jesus (Lumen Gentium, n. 58). Her role with Jesus was not passive. Pope John Paul II teaches, that at the foot of the Cross of our Savior, Mary's intense sufferings, united with those of her Son, were "also a contribution to the Redemption of us all" (Salvifici Doloris, n. 25). Because of this intimate sharing in the redemption accomplished by the Lord, the Mother of the Redeemer is uniquely and rightly referred to as "Advocate, Auxiliatrix, Adjutrix, and Mediatrix" (LG 62).

When the Church invokes Mary under the title, "Coredemptrix", she means that Mary uniquely participated in the redemption of the human family by Jesus Christ, our Lord and Savior.

Four Marian doctrines have already been defined as dogmas of Catholic truth: the Motherhood of God, the Immaculate Conception, the Perpetual Virginity of Mary, and her glorious Assumption into heaven.

Catechism of the Catholic Church: 963.
Bible: Jn 2:1-11; 19:26-27 Mark 335; Luke 2:19,51; 11:27-28.

Questions to answer:

1. Give three examples from the Bible where it is manifested that Jesus and Mary are inseparable.
2. How is Mary the perfect image of what the Church is and will be?
3. How is Mary the Mother of the Church?
4. What were the first four dogmas of faith solemnly defined concerning Mary?
5 What is the meaning of the Marian doctrine that speaks of her as Coredemptrix?

POINTS FOR PARENTS AND TEACHERS

Vatican Council II spoke gloriously of Mary. The eighth and final chapter of its Dogmatic Constitution on the Church, Lumen Gentium, *is dedicated to "The Role of the Blessed Virgin Mary, Mother of God, in the Mystery of Christ and the Church."*

The General Catechical Directory *also speaks of Mary as: full of grace, Model of the Church and Mother of God. This Directory was issued by the Sacred Congregation for the Clergy on April 11, 1971, and was confirmed by the Supreme Pontiff Paul*

VI, and ordered to be published by his authority.

On February 2, 1974, Pope Paul VI issued the famous Apostolic Exhortation, Marialis Cultus, *in which he strongly recommended the recitation of the family Rosary and encouraged the faithful to pray the Angelus. This succinct exhortation presents a beautiful summary of the Church's teaching on "Devotion to the Blessed Virgin Mary. " Prior to its publication, the Bishops of the United States gave similar instructions in an abbreviated form in their document,* Basic Teachings for Catholic Religious Education.

Because a solid devotion to Mary is essential for a well-balanced Catholic Christian life, parents and teachers must instill in today's youth a correct understanding and appreciation of God's Mother. Educators should study and use as resource material the documents mentioned above. These can be obtained for a nominal price from: Publications Office, United States Catholic Conference, 1312 Massachusetts Ave. NW, Washington, D.C. 20005.

LESSON 10
THE COMMUNION OF SAINTS

The Communion of Saints is really Christ's Mystical Body, the Church. It is made up of the faithful on earth, the saints in heaven and the souls in purgatory. This Family of God is united in grace with Jesus Christ, its Head.

Our Lord compared His Church to a plant, saying that He was the vine and we, its branches. The life-giving sap which flows through every living member of God's Family is sanctifying grace. This divine life comes through the action of the Third Person of the Blessed Trinity, the Holy Spirit, Who is the Soul of the Church.

Although some souls have more grace than others, God's life in each is the same, whether that person be on earth, in purgatory or in heaven. By sharing in the divine life, the members of the Communion of Saints are bound together as God's Family and as such are in union or "communion" with each other.

The Church Militant, Christ's Mystical Body on earth, looks longingly to heaven because there its members will see God face to face and be united with Him forever. Because God is so beautiful, powerful, mighty and good, it is impossible for men to understand or describe Him as He is or even to imagine what happiness will be theirs in the eternal home God has prepared for those who love Him.

The Communion of Saints:
The Church Militant… Triumphant… Suffering.

Jesus has commanded men to love one another. There are many different ways by which love can be expressed—prayer, good works, alms, sacrifices, etc. When a soul enters heaven, it joins the company of God's dearest friends and its power to love, show concern and pray becomes greater.

The blessed in heaven (called saints or the Church Triumphant) sincerely love and pray for all God's Family. Therefore, it is most fitting that the faithful on earth should often ask their assistance. Jesus, Who is the Head of the entire Communion of Saints, listens attentively to the blessed who stand before His eternal throne. Although men should love, honor and respect the entire Church Triumphant, they should have a particular devotion to their own patron saint and other saints to whom they feel especially attracted.

The third and final part of God's Family is the Church Suffering or the souls in purgatory. The Bible speaks of the EVERLASTING FIRES of HELL, which persons must suffer if they die without grace. But God in His justice, mercy and love allows souls who are not perfect at death to become pure and holy in purgatory. Although the members of the Church Suffering must endure terrible pains, they patiently accept these in hope and love, for their sufferings are not like the damned whose punishment is eternal and borne in hate.

Although the souls in purgatory can and do pray for others, they look for assistance from the Church Militant and Triumphant because they cannot help themselves. Both the saints in heaven and the faithful on earth can pray for their suffering brethren; but only the Church Militant can offer good works, fasting and Masses. Thus, it is through the Communion of Saints that men share in the divine life and imitate Christ by loving and helping each other.

All men should strive to be prepared for the Particular Judgment which takes place at the moment of death, Only those who die in the state of grace will be able to advance from the Church Militant to the Church Suffering or Triumphant. Then after the General Judgment at the end of the world, there will still remain only one Church; but all its members will be joined together with God in perfect and everlasting happiness and peace.

●●●

REVIEW QUESTIONS

1. What is meant by "the Communion of Saints"?

The Communion of Saints is Christ's Mystical Body, the Church. It is made up of the faithful on earth, the blessed in heaven and the suffering souls in purgatory. All members of God's Family are united by grace with their Head, Jesus Christ.

In the Apostles' Creed, the word "saints" means "holy ones." Although all members of Christ's Body are made "holy" at Baptism, only the blessed in heaven possess perfect holiness.

2. Can members of the Communion of Saints help one another?

Yes, members of the Communion of Saints can and should help one another. The blessed in heaven can pray for and help the souls in purgatory and the faithful on earth. The suffering souls in purgatory are able to pray for the faithful on earth, but cannot help themselves. Members of the Church Militant can relieve the suffering souls in purgatory by offering Masses, indulgences, prayers, sacrifices and good works for their intentions. They should also honor the saints in heaven and frequently beg their prayers for the souls in purgatory and the living on earth. Finally, the faithful should assist their fellowmen by the performance of the Spiritual and Corporal Works of Mercy.

DISCUSSION QUESTIONS

1. Does the word "saints" refer only to the blessed in heaven?

2. How are the blessed in heaven, the souls in purgatory and the faithful on earth joined together into one Family of God?

3. How can the members of the Communion of Saints help one another?

4. How does the suffering of the souls in purgatory differ from the suffering of the damned in hell?

5. Are the souls in hell part of the Communion of Saints? Explain.

6. What is meant by the Particular Judgment? When will this take place?

7. What is meant by the General Judgment? When will this take place?

8. Do the prayers and honor given to the saints take away from the glory due to God? Explain.

●●●

FOR OLDER STUDENTS

In the Apostles' Creed we confess our faith in "the communion of saints" immediately after confessing faith in "the holy Catholic Church." The communion of saints is the Church. It means a union among holy persons in holy gifts. The union is primarily in Jesus Christ, the Life and Light of the world.

All the spiritual goods of the Church as a common fund belong to all members. Since all members form one body in Christ, the good of each member is communicated to all others. The most important member of the Church is its Head, Jesus Christ, with His riches communicated to all members, through the Sacraments. When the faithful who are in the state of sanctifying grace eat and drink the Lord's body and blood in Holy Communion they grow in the communion of the Holy Spirit. They are thus aided supernaturally to communicate Jesus Christ to the world.

St. Paul speaks clearly in the Bible of our union and sharing with one another in the Church: "If one member suffers, all suffer together; if one member is honored, all rejoice together. Now you are the body of Christ and individually members of it" 1 Cor 12:26-27.

Every prayer and good work done in charity is for the good of the entire communion of saints. Each sin committed by any member of the Church is harmful to this communion. A great saint at any time in history is good for the entire Church to strengthen and upbuild it.

We can understand then that whenever any member of the Church has a special charism it is for the good of the entire Church. "To each is given the manifestation of the Spirit for the common good" (1 Cor 12:7).

There are three states of the Church. Some are pilgrims on earth. Other are being purified after death. Others are already in the glory of heaven. The saints in heaven have special intercessory power with the Father as they are more closely united to Jesus Christ in heaven. Their prayers still go to the Father through Christ in heaven.

Since the first days of the Church instituted by Jesus, Christ Christians have always honored the memory of the dead, praying for them. The Catechism of the Catholic Church says: "Our prayer for them is capable not only of helping them, but also of making their intercession for us effective." (958)

Catechism of the Catholic Church: 946-960.
Bible: Acts 2:42; Rom 14:7; 1 Cor 12:26-27; 10:24; 13:5; 1 Cor 15:26-27; 1 Tim 2:5; Eph 4:1-6.

Questions to answer:

1. Explain why in the Church the good of each member is communicated to all the members.

2. If the good of each member of the Church helps all the members what does sin do?

3. What are the three states of the Church and why are they so named?

●●●

POINTS FOR PARENTS AND TEACHERS

Young Catholics should be taught that God is glorified in His saints when they intercede for us. They should also thoroughly understand that there is no such thing as going to God without the help of the Mediator, Jesus Christ. Although Christ is truly God, we approach the Infinite through His humanity. Just as Jesus is "King of Saints," Mary is "Queen of Saints."

There are greater and lesser saints before the throne of God. Whenever we invoke the blessed in heaven to intercede for us, God is even more glorified, because then there are several individuals approaching God through Christ and honoring Him by prayer.

Young Catholics should be encouraged to pray for the souls in purgatory. The family Rosary, evening prayers, etc., can easily be concluded with the prayer: "Eternal rest grant unto them, O Lord. . ."

It is necessary that children learn the following very early in life:

1. *We are members of a supernatural organism, the Church—Christ's Mystical Body.*
2. *God's Family reaches beyond this world and includes the suffering in purgatory and the blessed in heaven.*
3. *We are joined in the fellowship of the saints even during our life on earth.*

Young Catholics will cease to perceive and judge the Church according to human terms and natural circumstances and will comprehend and appreciate its divine nature only when they correctly understand the supernatural character of authentic Christian living. They must constantly be reminded that we are a pilgrim people journeying to heaven, our only true and lasting home. When such concepts have been established, our youth will be able to understand that the Church was not ESSENTIALLY founded to relieve earthly sufferings or make the world a better place in which to live. Even though such goals are good and may even be considered necessary and Christian, the Church was primarily established to lead its members to heaven and eternal union with God.

"Eternal rest grant unto them O Lord, and let perpetual light shine upon them. "

LESSON 11
THE SACRAMENTS
ARE ACTS OF JESUS

The sacraments are acts of Jesus extended in time and space. Before Our Lord ascended into heaven, He instituted the seven sacraments and gave them to His Church.

Whenever and wherever a true sacrament is administered, Christ is present and acts in His power. For example, at Baptism, it is Jesus Who baptizes. It is likewise Jesus Who forgives sins through the Sacrament of Penance, just as it is He Who offers Himself to the Eternal Father in every Holy Sacrifice of the Mass. Thus through the sacraments, Christ continues to do throughout the centuries what He did when He lived on earth in His physical body almost 2,000 years ago.

A validly ordained priest or bishop is needed for most of the sacraments. Whenever a Catholic priest or bishop administers a sacrament, the very PERSON and POWER of Christ are present to give worship to God and grace to souls.

When Jesus lived on earth, men could actually see Him perform miracles of grace and nature. Although we cannot do this today, we can see and hear the outward signs used in the sacraments of the Church. To men of faith, these signs of water, oil, bread, wine, words and actions tell of Jesus' PERSON, POWER and PRESENCE which continue to give grace to men.

When the sacraments are administered, a person without

faith merely hears words or sees actions or objects. However, the believing Catholic Christian KNOWS that Christ is giving grace. Because the power of the sacraments depends solely upon Christ and not upon men, Jesus is present and acts in them whether one chooses to believe this or not. But in order to receive grace from the sacraments and give worthy homage to God, men must have faith, desire to receive grace and want to glorify God.

Normally, bread and wine are food for man's body. However, when these are changed into Christ's Body, Blood, Soul and Divinity at the Holy Sacrifice of the Mass, they become FOOD for his SOUL.

Water cleanses, refreshes and is necessary for life. In Baptism, it becomes the sign of Christ's PERSON, POWER and PRESENCE. In this sacrament, Jesus washes away all stains of sin from the soul and fills it with His own life of grace.

When the priest says, "I absolve you from your sins," in the Sacrament of Penance, he brings the very POWER and PERSON of Jesus into the confessional. In this sacrament, Jesus in the priest truly forgives sins and grants grace.

The seven sacraments are holy and must be received worthily. Each gives two types of grace: sanctifying grace and sacramental grace. Sacramental grace helps men carry out the particular purpose of the sacrament.

Our Lord instituted the Sacraments of Baptism and Penance to give God's life to souls spiritually dead through sin. These sacraments are called sacraments of the dead because Catholics do NOT have to be in the state of sanctifying grace to receive them worthily.

The Sacraments of Confirmation, Holy Eucharist,

The sacraments are acts of Jesus Christ
extended in time and space.
Each of the seven sacraments
has outward signs.

Anointing of the Sick, Holy Orders and Matrimony are called sacraments of the living. Persons must be in the state of sanctifying grace to receive them worthily. The chief purpose of these sacraments is to increase grace.

To summarize:

- The SEVEN sacraments of the Church are OUTWARD SIGNS.
- Each was made by Jesus Christ.
- Each is an act of Jesus Christ.
- Each gives glory to God and grace to men.

REVIEW QUESTIONS

1. What are the sacraments of the Church?

The sacraments of the Church are acts of Jesus Christ extended in time and space. They were instituted by Christ to give grace. The seven sacraments have outward signs which show those who believe that Christ is acting in His PERSON, POWER and PRESENCE whenever any true sacrament is administered.

2. Do all the sacraments give grace?

Yes, all the sacraments give grace if they are received with the right dispositions. In addition to sanctifying grace, each sacrament also gives a special grace, called sacramental grace, which helps men carry out the particular purpose of the sacrament.

3. What sacraments can be worthily received by persons who are not in the state of grace?

The Sacraments of Baptism and Penance (Confession) can be received by persons who are not in the state of grace.

4. What sacraments must be received only by persons in the state of grace?

The Sacraments of Confirmation, Holy Eucharist, Anointing of the Sick, Holy Orders and Matrimony must be received only by persons who are in the state of grace because these sacraments were instituted to increase grace and give glory to God.

DISCUSSION QUESTIONS

1. In your own words, explain what a sacrament is.
2. Who established the seven sacraments?
3. What is an "outward sign"?
4. How are the sacraments "outward signs"?
5. What types of grace do each of the sacraments give? Explain each.
6. Name some things Jesus did when He lived on earth nearly 2,000 years ago that He continues to do today.
7. Do the sacraments always give grace? Explain.

●●●

FOR OLDER STUDENTS

The Council of Trent (1547 A.D.) professed that Jesus Christ our Lord instituted all seven sacraments. The seven sacraments in the Church are: Baptism, Confirmation, Holy Eucharist, Penance, Anointing of the Sick, Holy Orders, and Matrimony.

The sacraments bring us forgiveness of sin and the grace of salvation which Jesus merited for us by the mysteries of His life. They also contain power to glorify the Father as the Holy Spirit acts in the sacraments through Jesus Christ who merited the grace which the Sacraments bring when offered or received with proper dispositions of heart.

The Council of Trent emphasized the unique character of Christ's sacrifice on the Cross as "the source of eternal salvation" (Heb 5:9) and taught that "his most holy Passion on the wood of the cross merited justification for us."

All that Jesus said and did while upon earth had saving power. This was true even during the hidden life of Jesus as well as His public ministry. The words and actions of Jesus throughout His entire life were salvific by way of anticipation of the power of the Paschal mystery. The mysteries of His life were all climaxed with His redemptive death on the Cross which brought us justification.

People who came into physical contact with Jesus Christ, who called Himself "the Way, the Truth and the Life," and also the "Light of the World," were often, if they were properly disposed in mind and heart, converted from sin and drawn to God the Father by receiving life in Jesus Christ. We encounter the same Jesus today in His Church through the seven sacraments.

The mysteries of the life of Christ contained power that Jesus would dispense through the sacraments during the centuries until the end of the world. Pope St. Leo the Great put it this way, "what was visible in our Savior has passed over into his mysteries." Each one of the sacraments has something visible about it and when administered by ministers or priests of His Church contain the power of Jesus Christ to cause what they signify.

To give examples of the signs of the sacraments: Water is a sign of life and washing clean. In Baptism the soul is washed clean of sin and given a share in the life of God for the first time. Bread and wine are the signs used in the Holy Eucharist. These foods changed into the Body and Blood of Jesus Christ give nourishment of divine life to our souls as bread and wine nourish natural life in the body. Each sacramental sign which the body experiences causes a supernatural effect in the soul. Just as the Church in early centuries had to determine the canon of Sacred Scripture, that is, which writings were truly inspired of the Holy Spirit, so the Holy Spirit who guides the Church "into all truth" brought the Church gradually to recognize that in liturgical celebrations there are seven such celebrations which are truly sacraments. The Church did not institute any sacrament. All seven were received from Jesus Christ. The Church in time clearly defined the meaning of each sacrament given the Church by Jesus Christ.

The Church herself is the Great Sacrament. This does not mean an eighth sacrament. Rather, since the Church is the Mystical Body of Christ, Jesus through His Church acts in seven special ways in the sacraments to dispense the power of His divine mysteries.

The Church forms "as it were, one mystical person" with

Christ the head, Jesus Christ. Whenever a sacrament is administered a priestly act takes place for a specific purpose as the
Church forms a priestly people. The apostles who received the
fullness of Christ's priestly powers received the Spirit of Jesus
to act in the name and person of Jesus in the sacraments. This
has been passed on to the successors of the apostles, the bishops and priests today.

The sacraments have the power to sanctify men, build up
the Body of Christ, the Church, and give worship to God the
Father, in, with and through Jesus Christ.

They presuppose faith but at the same time strengthen
faith.

The very rites of administering the sacraments instruct us
in the faith.

Whenever the Church celebrates a sacrament, she is confessing the same faith received from the apostles. The liturgical
life of the Church which revolves around the sacraments, especially the Eucharistic sacrifice, expresses what is the faith of the
Church. An ancient way of stating this truth is: "The law of
prayer is the law of faith."

No priest or the community may ever modify or manipu-
late the rite of any sacrament. Even the supreme Pontiff may
not change the liturgy arbitrarily. Each sacrament must always
be administered in the obedience of faith and with respect for
the mystery of faith and power contained therein as Jesus gave
it to His Church. Believers who live under the New Covenant
of Jesus Christ cannot be saved without the sacraments. Jesus,
through the power of the Holy Spirit comes to members of the
Church with His saving grace through the sacraments. The
fruit of any of the sacraments is that the Spirit of adoption
makes the recipients partakers in the divine nature, bring them

into an ever increasing living union with Jesus Christ.

Catechism of the Catholic Church: 615-618; 1113-1134.
Bible: Rom 5:19; Isa 53:10-12; Jn 9:12; 9:5; 14:6; 20:21-23;
Lk 5:17; 6:19; 8:46; 24:47; Mt 28:18-20; 2 Pet 1:4; 1 Cor
11;26; 15-28; 16:22.

Questions to answer:

1. What are three things the sacraments do?
2. When did the life of Jesus begin to have saving power for mankind?
3. Is man lacking anything in the Church today which was available to those who came into physical contact with Jesus when He was upon earth for 33 years?
4. Can we be saved without the sacraments?

POINTS FOR PARENTS AND TEACHERS

It is necessary that young people realize that Jesus Christ is as truly present in His PERSON and POWER in the sacraments of the Church today as He was during His life some 2,000 years ago.

Although it is correct to call the sacraments "channels of grace," Catholics must understand that these are NOT impersonal means by which God shares His life with men. Indeed, every time a person receives a sacrament, he really comes into an intimate union and contact with Christ. Therefore, to refer to the sacra-

ments as "acts of Jesus extended in time and space" is both correct
and forceful.

Young Catholics must understand the following important
truths of their faith. Parents and teachers should explain these concepts in simple, meaningful words and review them periodically.

- Catholics meet Jesus Christ Himself in the sacraments.
- Catholics should have a profound reverence for each of the
  sacraments.
- Catholics should receive the Sacraments of Penance and
  Holy Eucharist as often as possible.
- Catholics should not consider the sacraments as "fearful
  signs." Rather, they should perceive them as Jesus' acts of
  mercy and love.

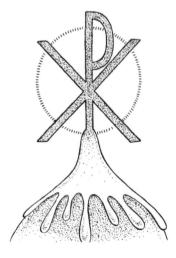

Jesus acts in the seven sacraments
of the Church
and gives grace to souls.

LESSON 12
THE HOLY SACRIFICE
OF THE MASS

The Holy Sacrifice of the Mass is the Church's greatest prayer. In it, Jesus Christ becomes present and offers Himself in love to the Father as He did on the Cross almost 2,000 years ago.

Although the Sacrifice of the Mass and Jesus' Sacrifice on Calvary are the SAME, there are important DIFFERENCES in these two actions of Christ. On the Cross, Our Lord offered Himself in a BLOODY MANNER; whereas, in the Holy Mass, He offers Himself in an UNBLOODY MANNER. This in no way implies that Jesus' Blood is no longer present at the Holy Sacrifice of the Mass. It simply means that Jesus chooses to act in a different way at Mass than He did on the Cross.

Although the Holy Sacrifice truly perpetuates Jesus' death, Our Lord no longer suffers pain or dies the physical death He did on the first Good Friday. Despite this fact, the Mass is not merely a ceremony intended to remind us of Jesus' death; rather, it is Christ perpetuating His offering on the Cross throughout time. Catholics firmly believe this mystery of faith because God has revealed it, although it is something they cannot fully understand.

When people attend Holy Mass, what is it they actually see? They see the priest officiating and the people participating. And what does the Eternal Father see? He sees His beloved Son, Jesus Christ, offering His death on the Cross for the redemption of the world. Indeed, human eyes cannot see

Through the ministry of priests,
Jesus Christ perpetuates His Sacrifice
on Calvary at every Holy Sacrifice
of the Mass.

Christ's Body and Blood, but they can see the signs of bread and wine and believe in faith that the real Body and Blood of Christ are present under these appearances.

Yes, Christ is really living and acting today under many visible signs. His PERSON and POWER are particularly present in every true sacrament. Within the Holy Sacrifice of the Mass, Our Lord reveals Himself to us in the great Sacrament of His Love, the Holy Eucharist. Through this sacrament, which is both a sacrifice and food for men's souls, Christ offers Himself through the signs of bread and wine as a Victim and perpetuates what He did on the Cross. Thus, Jesus Christ on Calvary and Jesus Christ in the Mass is one and the same Victim and Priest.

The Holy Sacrifice of the Mass is certainly the world's greatest and most powerful prayer. No other worship can compare with it. Should thousands of people pray fervently without distraction or interruption for millions of years, their combined efforts would in no way even begin to equal the value of but one Holy Mass. And why is this so? Because the God-Man, Jesus Christ Himself, offers and is offered in this sublime act of worship, making the Mass INFINITE in value.

It is for this reason that Holy Mother Church requires all Catholics from the age of seven years on to worship God each Sunday and Holy Day by participating at Mass. Only SERIOUS REASONS, such as sickness, great distance, etc., would excuse one from this obligation. Because it is sinful for Catholics to miss Mass deliberately on such days, they should take their responsibility seriously. At the same time, they should rejoice at the privilege which is theirs; for through the Holy Sacrifice of the Mass, they can offer themselves in union with Jesus as an acceptable sacrifice to the heavenly Father.

REVIEW QUESTIONS

1. What is the Sacrifice of the Mass?

"The Sacrifice of the Mass is not merely a rite commemorating a past sacrifice. In it, through the ministry of priests, Christ perpetuates the Sacrifice of the Cross in an unbloody manner through the course of the centuries. In it, too, He nourishes the faithful with Himself, the Bread of Life, in order that, filled with love of God and neighbor, they may become more and more a people acceptable to God." *General Catechetical Directory* of Rome and the American Bishops' *Basic Teachings for Catholic Religious Education.*

2. What is a sacrifice?

A sacrifice is the offering of a victim to God by a priest. In order that God be acknowledged as the Creator of all things, the victim must be destroyed in some way.

On the Cross, Jesus offered Himself to God the Father for our salvation and was both Victim and Priest. He continues to perpetuate His Sacrifice on Calvary in every Mass, although He does this in a different manner.

3. Must Catholics attend Mass every Sunday and Holy Day of Obligation?

Yes, Catholics must attend Mass every Sunday and Holy Day of Obligation. This law of the Church is based on the Third Commandment of God. Therefore, it is considered a serious failing if Catholics do not abide by this rule.

The American Bishops in their document, *Basic Teachings for Catholic Religious Education*, stated that it was a duty "...expected of Catholic Christians...to keep holy the day of the Lord's Resurrection: to worship God by participating in Mass every Sunday and Holy Day of Obligation...."

4. Who offered the first Mass?

Jesus Christ offered the first Mass at the Last Supper on Holy Thursday, the night before He died on the Cross.

DISCUSSION QUESTIONS

1. Could any number of private prayers ever equal one Holy Mass? Explain.

2. How is the Sacrifice of the Mass the same as Jesus' Sacrifice on Calvary? How do they differ?

3. Is Jesus Christ, Body, Blood, Soul and Divinity, truly present on the altar after the Consecration of the Mass? Explain.

4. Why is the Holy Mass called the unbloody sacrifice of Jesus Christ?

5. Who was the chief Victim and Priest at the Sacrifice on Calvary?

6. Who is the chief Victim and Priest in the Holy Sacrifice of the Mass?

7. Why is the Holy Sacrifice of the Mass the Church's greatest prayer?

8. Why is attendance at Mass on Sundays and Holy Days a serious obligation for Catholics?

●●●

FOR OLDER STUDENTS

The only perfectly pleasing sacrifice of worship given God the Father is the one that Jesus Christ offered on the cross for our salvation as a total offering to the Father's love. This sacrifice of the cross is perpetuated at the Sacrifice of the Mass today and is united to the heavenly liturgy. We can join in this offering each day.

Jesus chose the feast of the Passover to fulfill His promise that He would give His followers His Body to eat and His Blood to drink. The Holy Eucharist is more than a sacrament of the Lord's Body and Blood, Soul and Divinity for us to receive in Holy Communion; it is the Sacrifice of Jesus' death on the cross perpetuated when the divine liturgy of the Mass is offered. The Jewish Passover was given its definitive meaning by Jesus celebrating the Last Supper during the Passover meal. The Jewish Passover recalled the People of God being saved by the blood of the lamb the night the Angel of death passed over Egypt and thus the Israelites were able to pass out of Egypt, through the Red Sea toward the promised land. Each year the Jewish feast celebrated at the command of God the deliverance of the Jews from the bondage of Egypt. The deliverance was conditioned on the sacrifice of an unblemished lamb, bones unbroken, whose blood was used to sprinkle the doorpost of every Hebrew house on the night before their passage.

This deliverance of the Jews was a foreshadowing of the Christian Pasch when, through the sacrifice of Jesus Christ, the true Lamb of God, and the application of the merits of His blood, the human race was freed from the bondage of the devil and of sin.

In the early Church, Good Friday was called the Pasch of the Crucifixion, while Easter day was styled the Pasch of the Resurrection. The Paschal mystery of Jesus Christ's death on the cross and His passing over into life at the Resurrection is at the very center of the Good News that the apostles, and the Church ever since, are to proclaim to all the world.

When a validly ordained priest offers the Sacrifice of the Mass he is said to be celebrating the liturgy. The liturgy is essentially a divine work of the whole Christ, head and body. During a liturgical celebration, the whole assembly offers, each according to his own role. The baptismal priesthood of the whole Body of Christ enables those not ordained to offer too but only the man ordained through the sacrament of Holy Orders represents Christ as head and has the power to change bread and wine into the body and blood of Christ and perpetuate His sacrifice.

Only the ordained priest can bring about the Victim to be offered by all to God the Father.

There is also an eternal liturgy always taking place in heaven which the Spirit and the Church enable us to participate in whenever we celebrate the mystery of salvation in the sacrament.

The first part of the Mass is known as the Liturgy of the Word wherein the Word of God is proclaimed. The Liturgy of the Word is an integral part of sacramental celebrations. The Liturgy of the Eucharist follows wherein Jesus perpetuates His

Sacrifice and we participate in this divine offering of Jesus Christ to the Father. Finally we are able to receive our Lord in Holy Communion.Sunday, the day Jesus rose from the dead, is the pre-eminent day for the liturgical assembly, when the faithful gather to hear the Word of God and take part in the Eucharistic Sacrifice.

Catechism of the Catholic Church: 571 - 573;1136 - 1167.
Bible: Heb 9:26; Lk 24:26-27, 44-45; Heb 4:14-15: 10:19-Rev 4:5; 7:1-8.

Questions to answer:

1. What is the only perfect worship which can be given God the Father today?
2. Why is the Holy Eucharist called both Sacrifice and Sacrament?
3. What was the meaning of the Jewish Passover?
4. How does the Jewish Passover find its definitive meaning in the Sacrifice of the Eucharist which today we call the Mass?

●●●

POINTS FOR PARENTS AND TEACHERS

This lesson strongly emphasizes the sacrificial aspects of the Mass and Holy Eucharist. Although there is some validity to modern expressions such as, "the Mass is a celebration of life," etc.,

Catholics too often interpret these in exclusive or natural ways. Both the General Catechetical Directory *from Rome and the* Basic Teachings for Religious Education *of our American Bishops stress the Mass as "sacrifice. "*

Our young people should sense in faith that the Holy Mass is a mystery. The General Catechetical Directory *states:*

> *"It is not so much a man who celebrates the Eucharist as Christ Himself; for He it is Who offers Himself in the Sacrifice of the Mass by the ministry of the priests (cf Council of Trent, Decree on the Sacrifice of the Mass, Dz.-Sch., 1743). The sacramental action is, in the first place, the action of Christ, and the ministers of the Church are as His instruments."*

The General Catechetical Directory *approves of the word "perpetuates" when speaking of the Sacrifice of the Cross in an unbloody manner through the course of the centuries. Impress upon young Catholics the truth that each time they participate in Holy Mass, Jesus is perpetuating the self same sacrifice He offered on the Cross. It is our privilege to join Him in that offering today.*

*Jesus offers Himself to the Eternal Father
in an unbloody manner at every
Holy Sacrifice of the Mass.*

LESSON 13
BAPTISM:
OUR REBIRTH IN CHRIST

After His resurrection, Jesus told His Apostles: "Go...and make disciples of all nations, baptizing them in the name of the Father, and of the Son, and of the Holy Spirit" (Matt. 28:19). Indeed, it is necessary that all men be baptized if they wish to be saved, for Our Lord has said, "...unless a man be born again of water and the Spirit, he cannot enter into the kingdom of God" (John 3:5).

The great gift of sanctifying grace, which enables men to share in the life of God, is given to souls for the first time at Baptism. By this sacrament, men are spiritually "reborn," become adopted children of God and inherit the right to heaven.

Baptism can be received only once because it imprints an INDELIBLE MARK or CHARACTER on the soul. This mark is the SEAL of Christ and permanently signs men as "CHRISTIAN." Because it can never be erased, nothing, not even serious sin, can remove it. Thus, should a person be so unfortunate as to lose grace and be sentenced to the eternal fires of hell, he would still take the indelible mark of Christ received at Baptism to his place of eternal damnation.

At Baptism, Jesus Christ gives divine life to the soul and cleanses it from original sin. If a person is older when he is baptized, Christ in His POWER, PRESENCE and PERSON

At Baptism, Jesus Christ gives divine life
to the soul and cleanses it from
original sin and actual sin.

acts to forgive all the actual sins he has committed. Even the punishment due to personal sins is taken away, provided the newly baptized is sincerely sorry for having offended God.

However, Catholics must not think of Baptism merely as a sacrament that takes away sin. Indeed, it does more than that. In a positive way, Baptism brings special supernatural powers and gifts to the soul. For instance, it makes men members of Christ's Mystical Body, the Church, and grafts them like branches onto the divine vine, Jesus Christ.

The newly baptized are also sanctified (made holy) by the Holy Spirit, Who comes with the Father and Son to live in souls which have been restored to grace.

God gives the supernatural gifts of faith, hope and charity (love) at Baptism. These virtues continue to grow as men exercise them in their daily lives. By the gift of faith, men believe in God and accept Jesus Christ as their Lord and Savior and all the teachings of His Church.

Although the baptized can and often do lose sanctifying grace by serious sin, the virtues of faith and hope ever remain to help them regain divine life through the Sacrament of Penance. The right to receive Penance, as well as all the other sacraments of the Church, is still another privilege given to those who have been baptized.

Because Baptism is necessary for salvation, it is the serious duty of all Catholic parents to have their children baptized as soon as possible after birth. However, parental responsibilities do not end with Baptism. The supernatural graces given through this sacrament must be nourished in order to grow and be strengthened. For this reason, Holy Mother Church does not permit her priests to baptize infants or children unless parents solemnly promise to teach and form their offspring in the one true faith.

At Baptism, Catholics, personally or through their godparents, renounce Satan and all his pomps and works. By doing so, they take on the obligation of living the Christian life which means they must obey and imitate Christ and all who take His place on earth.

Although men use the God-life and supernatural gifts received at Baptism in this world, many of these gifts will continue to function throughout eternity as men adore the Blessed Trinity. Therefore, the baptized Catholic Christian should rightly proclaim, "I AM (not WAS) baptized," for he truly LIVES in Christ and the effects of this sacrament will last forever.

REVIEW QUESTIONS

1. What is Baptism?

Baptism is the sacrament of rebirth in Christ. Through it, men receive the gift of sanctifying grace for the first time and become God's adopted children and heirs of heaven. This sacrament cleanses the soul from original sin and all personal sins.

Through Baptism, men are "sanctified by the Spirit. . . (joined to) Jesus in his death and resurrection...(and welcomed) into the community of the Church. (This sacrament) permanently relates (the baptized) to God with a relationship that can never be erased. It joins him to the priestly, prophetic, and kingly works of Christ." *Basic Teachings for Catholic Religious Education.*

2. Why can Baptism be received only once?

Baptism can be received only once because the sacrament imprints a permanent character (mark) on the soul. Because this seal of Jesus Christ will last forever, it can never be erased and will be taken into eternity.

At Baptism, sanctifying grace and the supernatural virtues of faith, hope and charity are given to the soul. Although men can lose God's life by serious sin, the supernatural virtues of faith and hope ever remain to help men regain grace through the Sacrament of Penance.

3. Can an unbaptized person validly receive the other sacraments of the Church?

No, an unbaptized person cannot validly receive the other sacraments of the Church because it is only through Baptism that one becomes a member of Christ's Mystical Body, the Church. The indelible character received through Baptism gives men the power to receive the other sacraments.

DISCUSSION QUESTIONS

1. What supernatural gifts and powers are given to the soul at Baptism?

2. What sins are cleansed from the soul through the Sacrament of Baptism?

3. Why must persons be baptized before they can validly receive the other sacraments of the Church?

4. Explain what is meant by the statement: "Baptism grafts us like branches onto the vine."

5. Does the character of Baptism remain on the souls of persons eternally condemned to hell? Explain.

6. Why should Catholics speak of Baptism as a present happening and say, "I AM baptized," rather than refer to it as a past event by saying, "I WAS baptized"?

●●●

FOR OLDER STUDENTS

As a result of original sin inherited from Adam we enter the world deprived of original holiness and justice. Yet human nature is not totally corrupted. It is wounded in its natural powers. This means we are subject to ignorance, suffering, and death and have inclinations to evil which are called "concupiscence." While baptism imparts the grace of Jesus Christ, erases original sin, turns the person back toward God, yet, the consequences of human nature weakened by the fall remain and we must do battle with inclinations toward sin throughout life. Jesus required faith and baptism for the forgiveness of sin. Jesus Himself said baptism is necessary for salvation. (Jn3:5). A person later in life who makes a profession of faith while receiving Baptism is cleansed so fully and completely that absolutely nothing of sin remains, nor is there left any vestige or penalty due to forgiven sin remaining. The weakness of human nature, however remains.

Baptism is the first of the sacraments of Christian initiation which lays the foundation of every Christian's life, making one for the first time a "partaker of the divine nature," an heir with Jesus Christ, a temple of the Holy Spirit. Confirmation and the Eucharist are sacraments of initiation after Baptism which increase divine life in the soul and advance one toward the perfection of charity.

Baptism is the door to all the other sacraments of the Church as it not only frees us from sin but through it we are reborn as children of God and become members of Jesus Christ. This sacrament is called "the washing of regeneration and renewal by the Holy Spirit," Baptism makes one "a new creature," in Christ and an adopted son of God. The ordinary ministers of Baptism are the bishop, priest and deacon. In case of necessity, anyone can baptize. Even someone not baptized can baptize if they have the right intention to do what the Church does when she baptizes. The person must use the Trinitarian baptismal formula at the same time water is poured, namely, "I baptize you in the Name of the Father, and of the Son, and of the Holy Spirit."

The person who has been baptized receives the Word, "the true light that enlightens every man," (Jn 1:9; 1 Thess 5:5; Heb 10:32; Eph 5:8). The Church has always taught that those who die for the faith without the opportunity of Baptism by water are baptized in their death for and with Christ. It is called Baptism of blood.

Catechumens who are repentant of their sins and love God but who die having firmly desired Baptism but never had the opportunity receive Baptism of desire. Those who never receive any Christian instructions and remain ignorant of the Gospel of Jesus Christ and His Church, through no fault of their own, but during life seek truth and the will of God can be saved. It may be supposed that these would have desired Baptism explicitly had they known it was necessary for salvation.

The Church commends the souls of children to the mercy

of God who die without Baptism. We know that the infinite mercy of God desires the salvation of all. The Church hopes there is a way of salvation for these children. Some devout Catholics frequently make acts of desire for children who die without Baptism, such as those who are aborted.

The Church instructs that parents, sponsors, and the pastor are to see that a name is not given a child at baptism which is foreign to Christian sentiment. The sacrament is conferred "in the name of the Blessed Trinity" and since the Lord's name sanctifies man the Christian thus receives his name in the Church. It can be the name of a saint, a faithful follower of Christ, or express a Christian mystery or virtue. The Catechism of the Catholic Church instructs us that the name one receives is a name for eternity.

Catechism of the Catholic Church: 405; 978; 977-980; 1212 - 16; 1257-1274; 2156 - 2159.
Bible: Jn 3:5: Mk 16:15-16; Rom 6:4; 4:25; 2 Pet 1:4; 1 Cor 6:19; 12:23; Mt 28:19-20; Rev 2:17; 14:1; Eph 4:25.

Questions to answer:

1. Even though Baptism removes Original Sin from the soul what weaknesses remain after Baptism as a result of Original Sin?

2. If a person comes to faith later in life and is baptized what are the effects it has on the soul besides the removal of Original Sin and bestowing grace?

3. What is Baptism of desire and Baptism of blood?

4. Why should parents take great care in the kind of name they give their child?

POINTS FOR PARENTS AND TEACHERS

Parents and teachers must teach young Catholics that Baptism imprints an indelible character on the soul. This permanent seal of Christ gives the newly baptized the powers of Christ. Therefore, it is not simply a "beautiful" mark on the soul.

These truths become clearer as Catholics study Confirmation, the sacrament which "completes" Baptism, and as their awareness of the continuous aspects of Baptism grows. For example, the powers of this sacrament are used each time men worship God. This is particularly evident when Catholics participate in the great Sacrifice of the Mass, for then they glorify God the Father in, with and through Jesus Christ in the unity of the Holy Spirit.

Young Catholics should have a proper and complete understanding of Baptism. This means they must not limit their concept of it to the forgiveness of sin. They should realize that men are born without grace but receive it at Baptism. However, this sacrament does not remove the effects or consequences of sin. Men remain susceptible to the temptations of the world, flesh and devil after Baptism because they still have natural weaknesses which incline them to sin.

It is especially important that young Catholics in our contemporary society appreciate the serious responsibility parents assume when they have their offspring baptized. If parents are not prepared to profess their faith or undertake the duties of bringing up their children as Christians, the new rite of Baptism advises the parish priest to determine when infants can be baptized.

*At Confirmation, the baptized Christian
receives the seal of the Holy Spirit
as a gift of God the Father.*

LESSON 14
THE HOLY SPIRIT
AND CONFIRMATION

The Sacrament of Confirmation is an act of Jesus Christ which gives another indelible character to the soul. This seal of the Holy Spirit is a gift of God the Father. It should remind Christians that the Blessed Trinity is actively involved in their lives.

Although men are spiritually reborn at Baptism, they become more closely united to the Church by a new and special power of the Holy Spirit at Confirmation. This sacrament gives Catholics the necessary spiritual strength:

1. To witness for Christ and His Church.
2. To spread and defend their true faith.
3. To live authentic Catholic Christian lives.

By Baptism, men are initiated into three important roles of Jesus Christ. Jesus is Priest. Jesus is Prophet. Jesus is King (I Pet. 2:9).

As PRIEST, Jesus offered Himself in sacrifice on the Cross and became a bridge between God and man. As PROPHET, Jesus spoke for God in a human way and made known His word and will. As KING, Jesus rules over the hearts and wills of all men and nations, for He is King of kings (I Tim. 6:15). All authority comes from God. Jesus, the God-Man, has the highest authority in the Church; and He shares this with men, especially the Pope and bishops.

Catholics use the power of the indelible marks of Baptism and Confirmation in a special way at the Holy Sacrifice of the Mass. Although an ordained priest is needed at the altar, each member of the worshiping community offers the Victim Jesus to God the Father and truly shares in some way in the priesthood of Christ. Men are also united to Jesus the Priest when they present their daily prayers, works, joys and sufferings to God.

Catholics share in Jesus' role as PROPHET when they speak for Jesus and lead others to God by their good works, words and example. It is the grace of Baptism, strengthened by Confirmation, that gives men these great powers.

Although it may sometimes be difficult to understand how men share in Jesus' role as KING, it is easy to recognize this power in persons who have authority. The Pope, bishops, priests, parents, teachers, civil rulers, etc., all represent Christ as King. Therefore, those who refuse to obey lawful authority sin against Jesus the King. As representatives of God's authority, government officials must always use their power according to His laws.

Baptized and confirmed Catholics also permit the power of Jesus as King to act in them each time they participate at Holy Mass, pray, receive the sacraments or carry out any of their duties or responsibilities in Jesus' Name.

The Holy Spirit as the SOUL of the Church lives in every person who remains in the state of grace. He constantly inspires men to know, love and serve God. How much Christians should open their hearts to the "often-forgotten" Third Person of the Blessed Trinity in order that He can move them to pray and love God and all men! Catholics who are faithful to the inspirations of the Holy Spirit always:

1. Obey the Pope, their bishops and all lawful authority.

2. Love and appreciate the Holy Sacrifice of the Mass and the sacraments of the Church.

3. Grow more and more into the likeness of Jesus Christ, their Savior, Redeemer and God.

REVIEW QUESTIONS

1. Who is the Holy Spirit?

The Holy Spirit is God, the Third Person of the Blessed Trinity. He is equal to God the Father and to God the Son.

2. What does the Holy Spirit do for the salvation of souls?

The Holy Spirit, Who is the Soul of the Church, guides the Pope and the Catholic bishops of the world who are in union with the Pope to keep the Church in truth. He also gives Christians the strength to be good members of Christ and makes souls holy by living in them when they are in the state of grace.

3. What is Confirmation?

Confirmation is a sacrament by which baptized Christians receive the seal of the Holy Spirit as a gift of God the Father. This special sealing of the Holy Spirit gives Christians spiritual strength so they can:

1. Witness for Jesus and His Church in the world.

2. Spread and defend the true faith.

3. Live authentic Catholic Christian lives.

DISCUSSION QUESTIONS

1. Who gives the gift of the seal of the Holy Spirit to the soul in the Sacrament of Confirmation?

2. What special powers are given to men at Confirmation?

3. Are baptized and confirmed Catholic Christians obliged to spread the true faith? Explain.

4. Give specific examples to show how Catholics today can witness for Christ and defend their faith.

5. Explain Jesus' role as priest, prophet and king.

6. How can baptized, confirmed Catholics share in Jesus' role of priest, prophet and king?

7. How long will the special seal (or indelible character) given at Confirmation remain on the soul?

●●●

FOR OLDER STUDENTS

In the Latin Catholic rite the ordinary minister of Confirmation is the bishop. In the East, the priest who baptizes ordinarily confers Confirmation immediately in one and the same celebration. In the Latin Rite the priest confers Confirmation when he baptizes an adult or receives into full communion in the Catholic Church one who was baptized in another Christian community but which community did not have valid Confirmation. While the Bishop may for grave reasons concede to priests the faculty to administer Confirmation usually it is reserved for the Bishop as he is a successor of the apostles and has the fullness of the sacrament of Holy Orders. The administration by the bishop demonstrates that its effect is to unite one more closely to the Church, her apostolic origins and to her mission of witnessing for Jesus Christ.

Confirmation perfects Baptismal grace. It more deeply roots us as a Son of God and strengthens our bond with Christ and His Church.

Confirmation has the effect of giving the full outpouring of the Holy Spirit as once given the apostles at Pentecost.

The Church does not specify any special age when Confirmation should be received, but the person must have attained the age of reason, profess the Catholic faith, be in the state of sanctifying grace, and be prepared to be a disciple and witness to Jesus Christ, both in the community of the Church and the world. This assumes that some age and advanced instruction and formation in the Catholic faith has already taken place.

The person receiving Confirmation is anointed on the forehead with sacred chrism which was consecrated by the Bishop, together with the laying on of the minister's hand and the words: "Be sealed with the Gift of the Holy Spirit."

By anointing, the confirmed person receives the "mark," or seal of the Holy Spirit. Jesus Christ Himself said that He was marked with His Father's seal. (Jn 6:27). We are called Christians after Christ as we are sealed. "It is God who establishes us with you in Christ and has commissioned us; He has put His seal on us and given us His Spirit in our hearts as a guarantee." (2 Cor 1:21-22; Eph 1:13; 4,30)

Catechism of the Catholic Church: 1286-1321.
Bible: 2 Cor 2:15; Gen 38:18; 41:42; Jn 6:27; 2 Cor 1:21-22;
Eph 1:13:4, 30; Acts 1:14; Rom 8:15; Rev 7:2-3.

Questions to answer:

1. Why is Confirmation normally reserved for the Bishop?
2. What are the requirements for receiving Confirmation?
3. What evidence is in the Bible that Confirmation gives us not only the Holy Spirit but a supernatural seal for all eternity?
4. What are the Christian duties of one who has received the sacrament of Confirmation?

●●●

POINTS FOR PARENTS AND TEACHERS

The Holy Spirit has sometimes been called the "forgotten Spirit" because His role in the personal lives of men and the Church is often neglected or misunderstood.

Parents and educators should make young Catholics aware of the importance and necessity of the Holy Spirit in all spiritual acts. Many people have fallen prey to a serious error prevalent today which maintains that the Holy Spirit acts equally or in the same degree in every member of the Church. Although it is true that any validly baptized person who has the faith is "the Church," it is a misrepresentation of the teachings of Sacred Scripture and Catholic Doctrine to state that the Holy Spirit works as infallibly in each member of the Church as He does in its Magisterium.

There is another false teaching being promulgated in our times that also must be avoided. It proposes that Catholics are free to form their own Christian values after merely "considering" the opinion of the official Church because all possess the gift of the Holy Spirit. Catholic Christians who are truly committed to the holy Catholic Church MUST form their consciences according to the teachings of the Church—for Jesus promised it would always have the Holy Spirit to keep it in truth.

Adults instructing young Catholics about the Sacrament of Confirmation should make them realize that their duty as lay apostles consists in defending and spreading the faith.

Because of the errors prevalent in the world today, Catholic youth must be alerted to the fact that enemies, or at least misrepresentations of the true faith, can appear within, as well as outside, the Church. They must be prepared to recognize and reject any false teachers and teachings.

*The Holy Spirit comes to souls
in a new and special way
at Confirmation.*

LESSON 15
SIN IS AN OFFENSE AGAINST GOD

A person commits a sin if he deliberately chooses any thought, word, action, desire or omission that he knows is wrong. Morality comes from God's laws as they are made known through His lawful teachers. It does not come from society or from what others do, think or say.

When Our Lord appeared to St. Margaret Mary Alacoque and showed her His Most Sacred Heart, It was burning with the fire of divine love but surrounded and pierced by thorns. The thorns wounding Jesus' Heart represent sin, which is a direct offense against God.

When children disobey their parents' rules, it is not simply a case of a rule being broken. They truly offend their parents whose love and will are expressed in the rules they make. The same is also true in regard to God and His Commandments. When men sin, it is not merely a matter of some cold, lifeless law being broken. Men really fail in love and personally offend God each time they commit sin because the Ten Commandments and the laws of the Church represent God's tender love, concern and will.

All people, children and adults, are obliged to form their consciences correctly. To do so, they must study and learn what is right and wrong. Then they will be able to show they love God by doing only those things that please Him.

Now certain thoughts, words and actions are wrong, not because people decide this, but because they are in themselves wrong and God knows this to be true. Men can be sure they are forming their consciences correctly if they accept and obey the Ten Commandments, the laws of the Church and the teachings of the Pope and the bishops who are in union with him.

Above anyone else, the Vicar of Christ, our Holy Father in Rome, speaks for Jesus. Because God has given him the power and authority to make or change laws and to teach what is right and wrong, his words should be respected and obeyed. But neither the Pope nor the bishops can change the laws of God (the Ten Commandments) because they have no power over these.

Obviously, all sins are not equally grave; some are more serious than others. Although less serious sins, called venial sins, do not separate men from God by destroying His life in the soul, they do weaken men's will to love God.

Mortal sins are deadly, serious sins. They cause men to lose sanctifying grace and the right to everlasting happiness in heaven. But God is ever merciful and His love and grace are more powerful than sin. Therefore, He is always ready to draw sinners back into His friendship so they can love Him again.

Although it is possible for grade school children to commit mortal sins, it is not likely that they would do so. However, little children can and often do commit venial sins. Because every sin offends God, people, young and old, should be sorry for their sins and ask God's forgiveness for all their offenses, including less grave sins such as: saying bad words, being unkind, telling small lies, disobeying those in authority, etc.

Little children, like adults, have consciences and are able to

Jesus appeared to St. Margaret Mary
and showed her His Most Sacred Heart.
The thorns piercing the Heart of Jesus
are the sins of men.

learn right from wrong even when they are very young. It is a joy to hear second graders tell how eager they are to make their first Confession. Such children enjoy thinking and talking about Jesus' love, for they understand His mercy and infinite desire to forgive all who are sorry for their sins and ask God's pardon.

People of all ages are called to holiness. When St. Rose of Viterbo was only seven years old, she wanted to leave home and spend the rest of her life with God in prayer—but He had other plans. At the age of 12, St. Rose often took her cross, walked through the streets and preached to all she met. This saint constantly reminded others to do penance, return to religious practices and be totally obedient to the Pope.

St. Maria Goretti was another young saint who lived in our own modern times. Before she was 13 years old, she freely chose to die rather than commit a mortal sin. She learned and lived well the lesson she was taught before she received Jesus the first time in Holy Communion. She knew how to say "yes" to God and "no" to temptation. If all Christians would follow this teaching, they, too, would possess great peace and happiness on earth and someday join St. Maria Goretti and all the saints in the presence of God forever in heaven.

REVIEW QUESTIONS

1. What is sin?

Sin is any thought, desire, word, action or omission by which a person knowingly offends God. Every sin in some way involves breaking a moral law. By committing sin, a person fails to love God and do His will.

2. Are some sins more serious than others?

Yes, some sins, called mortal sins, are more serious than others.

A mortal sin separates the sinner from God and destroys sanctifying grace in his soul. If a person dies in the state of mortal sin, he cannot go to heaven; rather, he must spend his eternity in hell.

3. What are less serious sins called?

Less serious sins are called venial sins. These smaller sins should be avoided because they offend God and make the soul less pleasing to Him. A person who dies with venial sins on his soul will not go to hell, but he must suffer the fires of purgatory before he can enter heaven.

4. To commit a mortal sin, what three things are necessary?

To commit a mortal sin, three conditions are necessary:

1. The thought, desire, word, action or omission must be seriously wrong or considered seriously wrong.
2. The person must know the matter is seriously against the moral laws of God or the laws of His Church.
3. The person must deliberately and fully will to do the wrong.

5. What is an occasion of sin?

An occasion of sin is any person, place or thing that may easily lead one into sin.

There is a serious obligation to avoid the occasions of sin. To put oneself into such circumstances when they can be freely avoided is sinful in itself.

DISCUSSION QUESTIONS

1. Are certain thoughts, desires, words, actions or omissions wrong simply because an individual decides they are? Explain.

2. Who has the highest authority and responsibility in the Church for teaching and helping men form their consciences according to God's will? Explain.

3. Does a person sin if he deliberately places himself in the occasion of sin? Explain.

4. Name some specific occasions of sin that Catholics should avoid.

5. Give some examples of mortal sin. Explain why each sin is mortal.

6. Give some examples of venial sin. Explain why each sin is venial.

7. Should Catholics and all men avoid committing sin, even venial sin? Explain.

8. Why should we be willing to die rather than commit one deliberate mortal sin?

●●●

FOR OLDER STUDENTS

Sin is a failure in love for God and neighbor caused by attachments to what is contrary to the will of God. Sin offends reason, truth and right conscience. Sin is a revolt against God. Sin is opposed to the obedience of Jesus, our Savior. The root of sin is found in man's heart.

Sin is a personal free act contrary to God's love and for which we are responsible. One can be responsible for the sins of others by cooperating with them in any way, such as by praising or encouraging them, protecting evil-doers, etc.

Sin can be forgiven by turning to the mercy of God but to obtain His mercy, we must admit our failures. St. John the Apostle wrote: "If we say we have no sin, we deceive ourselves, and the truth is not in us. If we confess our sins, he is faithful and just, and will forgive our sins and cleanse us from all unrighteousness" (1 Jn 8-9). The mercy of God is infinite if we turn to Him in sorrow.

There are many kinds of sins. St. Paul in his Letter to the

Galatians wrote of the works of the flesh in contrast to the fruit of the Spirit: "Now the work of the flesh are plain: fornication, impurity, licentiousness, idolatry, sorcery, enmity, strife, jealousy, anger, selfishness, dissension, factions, envy, drunkenness, carousing, and the like. I warn you, as I warned you before, that those who do such things shall not inherit the Kingdom of God" (Gal 5:19-21).

While there are many kinds of sins the gravity of sin may be mortal or venial.Mortal sin is a grave violation of God's law, which turns man away from God and destroys charity in his heart. Venial sin does not remove grace or charity from the heart but it does offend or wound it. Mortal sin presupposes that the person guilty realized the serious sinful character of the act but acted in violation to God's will nonetheless. It removes one from the state of grace. One must then repent and seek God's forgiveness or face the consequence of exclusion from the kingdom of Christ and thus face eternal death in hell where there can be no repentance.

One who is ignorant of the seriousness of an act through no fault of his own is not held accountable before God. However, the principles of the moral law in general are written on the heart or conscience of every person. Each one has an obligation to become instructed in the true moral teachings of God and His Church and to accept the faith and morals of the Church in good conscience.

Venial sin impedes the soul's growth in Christian virtues. Frequent venial sin gradually disposes us toward mortal sin by weakening of the will. While venial sin does not deprive one of sanctifying grace and friendship with God, or the right to heaven, it does weaken charity. There are seven capital sins, so called, because they engender other sins: pride, avarice, envy, wrath, lust, gluttony, and sloth. Sins which cry to heaven are murder, sodomy, unjust oppression of people; refusing the cry of the foreigner, widower, and orphan in need of help; and injustice to the wage earner.

Catechism of the Catholic Church: 1731 - 1739; 1846 - 1869.
Bible: Gen 3:13; 4:10; Lk 15; Mt 1:21; 26:28; Rom 5:21; Phil 2:6-9; Mk 10:19; Ex 3:7-10; 20:10-22.

Questions to answer:

1. Why is sin an offense against right reason and right conscience?
2. How could one be responsible for the sins of others?
3. Does ignorance of the sinfulness of an act mean that it was alright to have done the wrong act? Explain answer.
4. While mortal sin deprives one of sanctifying grace what are the effects of venial sin?

●●●

POINTS FOR PARENTS AND TEACHERS

Our American Bishops in Basic Teachings for Catholic Religious Education *said:*
"Religious instruction must not be silent about the reality of sin, the kinds of sin and the degree of gravity and personal wilfulness which indicate mortal sin. Instruction must remind the student of the sufferings and the death on the cross which Christ endured to destroy the

effects of sin.

"But it must go on to speak eloquently of God's forgiveness. Even though a man sins, he can be pardoned.
The power of grace is greater than that of sin. The superabundant love of God restores the penitent and draws him
toward salvation.

"It is important that the awareness of sin not be lost
or lessened. The Christian must have clear knowledge of
right and wrong, so as to be able to choose with an
informed conscience to love God and avoid offending
him."

Our modern age of permissiveness tries to explain away sin.
Situation ethics and various forms of new moralities are a recur-
rence of "Modernism" which Pope St. Pius X condemned. These
theories are confusing many young people and adults today.
Catholic Christians should be guided by the Ten Commandments
and the precepts and teaching of God's Church. These laws clearly
define men's duties and responsibilities and enable them to do
God's will.

LESSON 16
THE SAINTS AND THE COMMANDMENTS OF GOD

Because the Ten Commandments are important, they should be memorized. But merely knowing them by heart is not enough. The laws of God must also be understood and lived. Jesus made this very clear when He said, "If you love me, keep my commandments" (John 14:15).

Many examples of moral living can be found in the *Bible* and *Lives of the Saints*. Two saints whom young people should certainly know about are St. John Bosco and St. Dominic Savio.

As a boy, John Bosco was saddened because some priests he knew never took time to talk with him. There were others, however, who always seemed ready to listen, answer questions and give advice when this was needed.

John Bosco became a priest when he grew up. During his priestly life, he wrote books, preached sermons, gave retreats, directed orchestras, heard confessions and formed organizations to help young people love God and keep His laws. He also established homes for poor boys and taught them their Catholic Faith and other important studies and skills.

Because he was always joyful and loving, John Bosco became known as the "smiling saint." In time, the boys also called him the "jolly marathoner" or "happy miler." Do you know why? Because at the age of 53, Father John could still outrun any boy under his care.

By word and example, St. John Bosco taught youth that REAL saints are happy. He also helped them realize they could keep the Commandments of God and the Church and still live beautiful lives, full of joy and youthful vigor. When he worked with boys, his teaching was, "Have lots of fun...but draw the line when it comes to sin."

Many of John Bosco's students were living when Pope Pius XI canonized him in 1934. They knew God had given their beloved Father many special graces and were happy when the Church honored him with the title of saint.

In 1862, John Bosco had a vision which seemed to portray the Church and the world in our own troublesome times. He saw the Church, represented by a ship, being fiercely attacked. In the threatening waters surrounding it were two large pillars. On one stood Our Blessed Lady, Help of Christians; on the other, a large Host representing Jesus in the Blessed Sacrament. The Ship of Christ with the Pope at its helm continued to be violently battered until the Holy Father succeeded in anchoring the Church firmly to the two pillars.

When this was done, the enemies fled, the attacks ceased and the Church peacefully sailed on in smooth, calm waters.

This vision reminds Catholics that Satan and his followers will continuously try to destroy Christ's Church. However, they will never succeed if Catholics:

1. Have a strong faith and reverence for Jesus in the Blessed Sacrament;
2. Are devoted to Mary; and
3. Remain loyal and obedient to the Vicar of Christ and the authentic teachings of the Church.

Dominic Savio was a pupil of John Bosco. He died when

he was only 15 years old. In 1954, Pope Pius XII officially declared Dominic a saint of the Church. Today he is known throughout the world as the patron of all Catholic boys and girls.

Dominic Savio learned to keep God's Commandments when he was very young, and he taught others to do the same. On the day of his first Communion, Dominic took as his motto, "Death rather than sin."

Our Lord had a special love for His youngest Apostle, St. John; and Father John Bosco had a "favorite son" in his young student, Dominic. Dominic Savio always gave good example. He straightened out fights and arguments, persuaded boys to burn bad pictures and books and told them not to use bad language. If any boys had not been to Confession for a long time, Dominic would encourage them to receive the Sacrament of Penance.

Dominic Savio advised young people to prove their love for God by obeying His laws and doing good. He urged his friends to do penance for their sins and to strive to please God in all their thoughts, words and actions. Even though he corrected others when they did wrong, Dominic Savio was never thought of as a "sissy." His life, courage and zeal inspired other boys to respect and admire him and to follow his advice and example.

Of course, there were times when Dominic found it difficult to obey God and do His will. However, by remaining firm in his efforts and beliefs, he became a great hero and saint. Modern youth should follow the example of St. Dominic Savio and seek his help so that they, too, may be faithful followers of Christ and loyal members of His Church.

God's laws must be understood and lived.

REVIEW QUESTIONS

1. What are the Ten Commandments of God?

The Ten Commandments of God are as follows:
1. I, the Lord, am your God. You shall not have other gods besides me.
2. You shall not take the name of the Lord, your God, in vain.
3. Remember to keep holy the sabbath day.
4. Honor your father and your mother.
5. You shall not kill.
6. You shall not commit adultery.
7. You shall not steal.
8. You shall not bear false witness against your neighbor.
9. You shall not covet your neighbor's wife.
10. You shall not covet anything that belongs to your neighbor.

(From: *Basic Teachings for Catholic Religious Education*, United States Bishops.)

2. What books present many examples of moral living?

The *Bible* and *Lives of the Saints* present many examples of moral living.

DISCUSSION QUESTIONS

1. Briefly tell the life of one saint and show how that person kept the Commandments of God.

2. In your own words, explain what each of the Ten Commandments means.

3. Name some sins that would not directly harm another person. Would these sins offend God? Explain.

4. What motto did St. Dominic Savio take on the day of his first Communion? Is this a good rule to follow? Explain.

5. Are saints happy? Explain.

6. Do saints have to overcome temptation and fight against sin? Explain.

7. What must Christians do to prove they really love God?

●●●

"If you love me,
keep my commandments. "
—John 14:15

FOR OLDER STUDENTS

The Ten Commandments reveal in their fundamental content grave obligations since they concern man's duty to God and neighbor. They cannot change but oblige always and everywhere. There is no dispensation from any of the Ten Commandments.

This does not mean that every offense against the Commandments is always a mortal sin. Circumstances or intentions can change the gravity of sin. By the first commandment we are obliged to believe, hope in and love God above all else. We must adore God alone, pray to him, offer Him worship. We must offer God authentic worship in the manner He has commanded. This first commandment forbids superstition, divination or magic. Christians are permitted to venerate icons, sacred images of holy persons and things which raise our hearts and minds to God.

The second commandment requires respect for the Lord's name which is holy. It forbids improper use of God's name. It forbids the offensive use of the name of God, Jesus Christ, the Virgin Mary or the saints. The third commandment: The Lord's day for Christians is Sunday and must be observed as a holy day. One must abstain from labors and business concerns which impede the worship to be rendered to God. Sunday is a day of proper relaxation of mind and body, a day of rest. We must avoid activities which demand labor of others to keep them from observing the Lord's Day.

The fourth commandment: After God we must honor our parents and all those who possess lawful authority exercised in God's name. When parents exercise their authority properly and it is respected by children this protects the well-being of family life and human and Christian society. Children also owe parents gratitude, just obedience, and assistance where needed. Parents are responsible for the education of children in faith, prayer and the virtues as well as physical needs. All must work with civil authority for the upbuilding of society in truth, justice, solidarity and freedom. But citizens must not follow civil authority when they pass laws against the moral order.

The fifth commandment: The murder of a human being is gravely against the dignity of the person and the holiness of the Creator. Sometimes defense is a grave duty in order to protect the lives of others or the common good.

From the moment of conception, the child has a right to human life. Deliberate abortion is a criminal act contrary to God's law. Automatic excommunication from the Church results from the mortal sin of abortion which requires, not only repentance, but permission of the bishop to receive absolution. The embryo must be treated like every other human being. Intentional euthanasia is murder. Suicide is seriously forbidden by the fifth commandment. Scandal is a grave sin when it influences others toward sin. We must do everything reasonably possible to avoid war. Arms race is a great curse on human society.

The sixth commandment: Each man and woman should accept their sexual identity, as man and woman were both equally given personal dignity by God. Every baptized person is called to live a chaste life according to his state in life. The sins gravely contrary to chastity include masturbation, fornication, pornography and homosexual practices. The covenant of married people imposes the obligation to work to keep their marriage indissoluble. Fecundity is good, a gift and end of marriage. Direct sterilization and contraception are contrary to the moral law. Grave offenses against marriage include adultery, divorce, polygamy and free union.

The seventh commandment: This commandment requires the practice of justice and charity toward property and fruits of others labor. Man has a right to private property. Theft is taking or using goods of others against their reasonable will. When there has been injustice in these ways reparation is required including restitution of stolen goods. Human beings may not be enslaved for commercial or totalitarian purposes. All must use the world's minerals, vegetable and animal resources of the world with the sense of moral obligations toward future generations. Economic and social life must respect the rights of all with due charity. Giving alms to the poor is both a work of charity and justice pleasing to God.

The eighth commandment: Truth must be shown in relationship to all. Respect for the reputation and honor of others forbids detraction and calumny in word or attitude. When a neighbor has the right to the truth it must always be spoken. Any offense against truth requires reparation. The Golden Rule will help one discern whether to reveal a certain truth to someone who requests it. Professional secrets must be kept which includes the sacramental seal of the confessional. Society has a right to information that is true but moderation and discipline by the social media should be practiced.

The ninth commandment: While the sixth commandment especially forbid sins against purity in action this ninth commandment specifies that one must be pure even in thought and desire. One must not even look upon another to whom one is not validly married with desire in one's heart to possess that person. This commandment forbids lust or consent to carnal concupiscence. The heart must be purified by practicing temperance. Purity of heart requires prayers, the practice of chastity, purity of intention. Modesty is required by this commandment, as regards dress and use of the eyes. Modesty protects the inner heart of a person.

The tenth commandment: This commandment forbids avarice or desire for riches and power. Envy is sadness at another's goods or talents. Envy is combatted through goodwill, humility and acceptance of divine providence. Detachment from riches in one's heart is necessary to enter the Kingdom of heaven.

Catechism of the Catholic Church: 2052 - 2557.
Bible: Exodus 20:1-17; Deuteronomy 5:6-22.

Questions to answer:

1. Why could the Church never dispense with any of the 10 Commandments?

2. Which of the commandments are directed especially to protect and promote the holiness of the family?

3. What is the difference between the sixth and the ninth commandment?

4. Which commandments give a positive demand and which give a negative demand?

POINTS FOR PARENTS AND TEACHERS

In Basic Teachings for Catholic Religious Education, *our Bishops stated:*

"…the student should know the Ten Commandments as part of his religious heritage….

"Towards God the Christian has a lifelong obligation of love and service. The Will of God must be put first in the scale of personal values…. One must have toward God the attitude of a son to an all-good, all-loving Father, and must never think or live as if independent of God. He must gladly give to God genuine worship and true prayer, both liturgical and private.

"Man must not put anyone and anything in place of God. This is idolatry, which has its variations in superstition, witchcraft, occultism…."

Father Fox, after consulting parents and young people, has made a cassette entitled "Teenagers and the Ten Commandments." On this tape, Father talks about each of the Ten Commandments. Attention is given to: attendance at Sunday Mass, respect for God's Name, stealing, purity, occultism, Satanism, etc. This tape sells for $4.50 and is available from: Pope Publications, Box 6161, San Rafael, CA 94903.

Jesus gave His Church AUTHORITY. He said those who obey it obey Him. As the successors of St. Peter and the first Apostles, the Pope and bishops have the power, right and responsibility to make laws for the Church and to change any laws it has made. They cannot, however, change any of God's laws.

When Catholics listen to and obey the teaching authority of Christ's Church, they are, in truth, listening to and obeying God. Therefore, to reject the Church is to reject Jesus; and to reject Jesus is to reject God the Father Who sent His Divine Son to redeem the world and found His Church.

The American Bishops have repeatedly reminded Catholics that they must obey the Precepts (laws) of the Church. Rome, meaning our Holy Father, the Pope, has agreed. The laws of the Church help Catholics know exactly what they must do to live in God's grace and obtain salvation according to the Gospels.

It is impossible to list all the general laws of the Church and the many particular laws of each diocese in this lesson. (A diocese is a territory of parishes which is ruled by a bishop.) However, the following Commandments of the Church are important and should be understood and practiced by all Catholics.

Jesus gave His Church AUTHORITY.
Those who are obedient to it
are obedient to Him.

Keep Holy the Day of the Lord's Resurrection

Christians keep Sunday as the Lord's Day instead of Saturday (which is the Jewish Sabbath) because Sunday is the day of Our Lord's Resurrection.

According to the Bible, the Lord's Day begins in the evening. For this reason, the Church has stated that Catholics may fulfill their Sunday Mass obligation by participating in the Holy Sacrifice of the Mass on Saturday evening.

It is a law of the Church that Catholics must assist at Mass EVERY SUNDAY and HOLY DAY of OBLIGATION. Therefore, those who say Catholics only have to attend Mass when they "feel like it" or when they "get something out of it" are seriously wrong. Such opinions should be ignored because they are not what God wills. Any Catholic who misses Mass on the Lord's Day through his own fault commits a serious sin.

However, attendance at Holy Mass is only one part of the Catholic Christian's duty. The Church clearly teaches that its members must also avoid all needless work, business activities, unnecessary shopping, etc.

Lead a Sacramental Life

Church law states that Catholics must confess their sins at least once a year and receive Holy Communion during Easter time. (Those Catholics who have no serious sins to confess are not obliged to go to Confession each year.) Although the reception of the Sacraments of Penance and Holy Eucharist once a year entitles Catholics to a Christian burial and is enough to keep them on parish records, it does little more.

Therefore, the Church says what Jesus wills—receive Holy Communion FREQUENTLY and go to Confession REGULARLY.

Observe the Marriage Laws of the Church

Because God Himself forbids remarriage after separation or divorce, the Church does the same. Marriage lasts until death. Furthermore, Church law still states that Catholics should marry Catholics. Mixed marriages (those marriages where one partner is not Catholic) demand a special permission which only bishops can give. Normally a priest must witness the marriage of a Catholic. This is so even in the case of an authorized mixed marriage.

Strengthen and Support the Church

Catholics are obliged to contribute to the support of the Church. This means they must give financial help to their Parish Church, to the worldwide Church and to the Holy Father in Rome. Children, too, should make regular, generous offerings to the Church. Those who do this as young Catholics will undoubtedly continue to fulfill this serious obligation as adults.

Do Penance

Jesus said men must do penance to save their souls. The American Bishops have told Catholics that FRIDAY is the weekly day of penance, and LENT the yearly season of penance. Thus the Church, through its bishops, reminds Catholics that they are obliged to make the Gospel teaching of penance an important part of their lives.

Have a Missionary Spirit

Before Our Lord ascended into heaven, He told His disciples to teach all nations. To do this, men must:

1. Know their religion.
2. Be able to present it correctly.

Since all Catholics are obliged to become missionaries for Christ and His Church, they should: study their faith, live it, share it with others and contribute to the support of missionaries who are teaching the true faith throughout the world.

REVIEW QUESTIONS

1. What are some of the specific duties of Catholics?
(The traditionally mentioned "Precepts of the Church" are marked with an asterisk.*)

1. To keep holy the day of the Lord's Resurrection: to worship God by participating in Mass every Sunday and Holy Day of Obligation: * to avoid those activities that would hinder renewal of soul and body, e.g., needless work and business activities, unnecessary shopping, etc.

2. To lead a sacramental life: to receive Holy

Communion frequently and the Sacrament of Penance regularly—

—minimally, to receive the Sacrament of Penance at least once a year (annual confession is obligatory only if serious sin is involved).*

—minimally, to receive Holy Communion at least once a year, between the First Sunday of Lent and Trinity Sunday.*

3. To study Catholic teaching in preparation for the Sacrament of Confirmation, to be confirmed, and then to continue to study and advance the cause of Christ.
4. To observe the marriage laws of the Church: * to give religious training (by example and word) to one's children; to use parish schools and religious education programs.
5. To strengthen and support the Church: * one's own parish community and parish priests; the worldwide Church and the Holy Father.
6. To do penance, including abstaining from meat and fasting from food on the appointed days.*
7. To join in the missionary spirit and apostolate of the Church.

(The preceding was taken from Appendix B of the United States Bishops' *Basic Teachings for Catholic Religious Education* which was approved by Rome.)

DISCUSSION QUESTIONS

1. Why is the authority of the Church really the authority of Jesus?

2. Using your own words, explain the duties of Catholic Christians in " keeping holy the day of the Lord's Resurrection."

3. What advice would you give to a Catholic who said, "I only have to go to Holy Communion once a year"?

4. Does a Catholic's obligation to study his faith stop at any special age? Explain.

5. When should Catholics begin contributing to the support of the Church? Why?

6. Why should boys and girls make sacrifices and do penance?

FOR OLDER STUDENTS

The Catechism of the Catholic Church states: "The precepts of the Church are set in the context of a moral life bound to and nourished by liturgical life. The obligatory character of these positive laws decreed by the pastoral authorities is meant to guarantee to the faithful the indispensable minimum in the spirit of prayer and moral effort, in the growth in love of God and neighbor." The Catechism for the universal Church presents us with the traditional six precepts of the Church in a positive manner so as to help us interpret the spirit of love and union with God and fellow members of the Church. The first precept states: "You shall attend Mass on Sundays and holy days of obligation". It explains that this first precept "requires the faithful to participate in the Eucharistic celebration when the Christian community gathers together on the day commemorating the Resurrection of the Lord." "To participate" means active participation in body and soul and heart, not mere physical attendance.

The second precept, "You shall confess your sins at least once a year", ensures worthy reception of the Holy Eucharist by the reception of the sacrament of Reconciliation (Confession). The sacrament of Reconciliation continues the work of conversion and forgiveness begun at Baptism.

The third precept, "(You shall humbly receive your Creator in Holy Communion at least during the Easter season", the Catechism says, "guarantees as a minimum the reception of the Lord's Body and Blood in connection with the Paschal feasts, the origin and center of the Christian liturgy."

The fourth precept, "You shall keep holy the holy days of obligation", the Catechism tells us "completes the Sunday observance by participation in the principal liturgical feasts which honor the mysteries of the Lord, the Virgin Mary, and the saints".

The fifth precept, "You shall observe the prescribed days of fasting and abstinence" – is not only to prepare us for the liturgical feasts but to strengthen us to achieve mastery over lower instincts and to attain freedom of heart.

Formerly the law of abstaining from meat on Fridays bound seriously on all Fridays of the year in the United States. At present, abstaining from meat binds seriously only on Ash Wednesday and the Fridays of Lent. However, the National Conference of Catholic Bishops in their pastoral statement on Penitential Observance for the Liturgical Year, when in 1966 they lifted the strict requirement concerning meat on all Fridays, mindful that Jesus Christ died for our salvation on Friday, added:

"Friday itself remains a special day of penitential observance throughout the year, a time when those who seek perfection will be mindful of their personal sins and the sins of mankind which they are called upon to help expiate in union with Christ Crucified. Friday should be in each week something of what Lent is in the entire year. For this reason we urge all to prepare for that weekly Easter that comes with each Sunday by freely making of every Friday a day of self-denial and mortification in prayerful remembrance of the passion of Jesus Christ."

The bishops no longer held Catholics to the traditional law of abstinence binding under pain of sin, as the sole prescribed means of observing Friday," yet, they added, "we give first place to abstinence from flesh meat. We do so in the hope that the Catholic community will ordinarily continue to abstain from meat by free choice as formerly we did in obedience to Church law.

"We shall thus freely and out of love for Christ Crucified show our solidarity with the generations of believers to whom this practice frequently became, especially in times of persecution and of great poverty, no mean evidence of fidelity to Christ and His Church."

If as Catholics we restrict penance to only 7 days, (Ash Wednesday and Fridays of Lent) we hardly observe the divine law that all the faithful are required to do penance.

We should consider it a matter of conscience normally to do some special penance each Friday of the year as well as during the time of Lent.

The 6th precept of the Church, in the Catechism of the Catholic Church, is now stated this way: "The faithful also have the duty of providing for the material needs of the Church, each according to his abilities."

Catholics should support according to their means, not only the local parish, but contribute to the Church at the wider levels, diocese, nation, the Holy Father and missions of the world.

There is the moral obligation, in addition to supporting the material needs of the Church, to assist in "building up the Church" by constant faith convictions and a good moral life. In this way they hasten the coming of the Reign of God. The precepts of the Church involves practical guidance from the Magisterium so that the faith and morals of the members of the Church are preserved and lived.

Catechism of the Catholic Church: 2041 - 2051.
Bible: Eph 4:13; Rom 12:8,11

Questions to answer:

1. Explain what is meant by the precepts of the Church set in the context of a moral life bound to and nourished by liturgical life.

2. The obligatory character of these positive laws decreed by the Church are directed to what purpose?

3. What is the present teaching of the Church as regards the observance of the Fridays of the year?

4. What is obliged by the sixth precept of the Church?

POINTS FOR PARENTS AND TEACHERS

This lesson presents the specific duties of Catholics as they are listed by the Bishops of the United States. It should help young people understand that their Catholic Faith not only helps them save their own souls, but it is also meant to be shared.

Since the Church is essentially missionary in spirit, its members have the responsibility of extending their faith. The obligation of being concerned about the salvation of other souls is developed again in Lesson 33 of this book, "A 10-Point Daily Spiritual Program."

Although the Church teaches that Catholics must obey the Commandments of God and the Precepts of the Church, it does not want its members to be guilty of "legalism." The dangers of legalism are obvious. Stressing strict conformity to the letter or form of the law is restrictive and neglects the more beautiful, positive aspects of the true Catholic Faith such as grace and the spirit of the law.

Young Catholics should understand the nature of the Church as Christ's Mystical Body and realize that everything the Church teaches and commands comes from Jesus Christ, Who is one with the Church. They should also know that obedience to the Precepts of the Church is a concrete expression of one's faith and love of God.

The Heart of Jesus wishes to be honored
along with the Immaculate Heart of Mary.
Make YOUR heart one with Theirs.

LESSON 18
JESUS FORGIVES SINS;
THE SACRAMENT OF PENANCE

When Jesus lived physically on earth nearly 2,000 years ago, He often spoke these comforting words to sinners: "Your sins are forgiven. Go in peace." Down through the centuries, Our Lord continues to do the same through His ordained priests in the Sacrament of Penance, which is sometimes called "Confession."

Yes, the very POWER and PERSON of Jesus are present and act each time a Catholic is truly sorry for his sins and humbly confesses them to a priest. When men are ordained to the priesthood, they receive, through the Sacrament of Holy Orders, an indelible MARK of Jesus on their souls. This character, which lasts forever, gives them the power to change ordinary bread and wine into the Body and Blood of the Lord and to forgive sins.

God, Who knows all things, realized men would sin and need pardon. Therefore, the Second Person of the Blessed Trinity, Jesus Christ, the God-Man, instituted a special sacrament, Penance, by which sins committed after Baptism could be forgiven. Sacramental Confession not only brings God's pardon, peace and grace to those who have fallen into serious sin, but it also makes the soul worthy to receive Our Lord in the Holy Eucharist. Because the Church realizes what tremendous benefits come from this sacrament (as well as its necessity

*Jesus Christ acts through His priests
to forgive sins in the Sacrament of Penance.*

in some cases), it states that those preparing to make their first Holy Communion should also learn about the Sacrament of Penance and be prepared to confess their sins.

Although sacramental Confession is NECESSARY only for persons who have committed mortal sin, it is also important and helpful for ALL Catholics, including those who are guilty of less serious offenses. In the Sacrament of Penance, Our Lord truly forgives men all their sins if they:

1. Are sorry for their offenses;
2. Confess all mortal sins and even include, as the Church recommends, troublesome and often-committed venial sins;
3. Resolve NOT to commit the same sins again; and
4. Are willing to do the acts of penance the priest gives.

In order to appreciate the power and beauty of Penance, Catholics must realize that this sacrament not only takes away sin; it also:

1. Restores or increases sanctifying grace;
2. Enables Catholics to regain the merits of their good works if these were lost by mortal sin;
3. Provides an opportunity for spiritual direction or advice; and
4. Takes away the ETERNAL punishment and at least part of the TEMPORAL punishment due to sin.

There are people today who say priests cannot forgive sins because they are merely men. Such remarks are not new. Even when Jesus lived, some doubted His power to pardon sinners and refused to accept Him as the Son of God.

Christians have always believed that God forgives sin and

gives grace at Baptism. Now, if God chooses to use man as His instrument in one sacrament, Baptism, can He not do the same in another? Of course—and this is precisely what He does in Confession. However, it should always be understood that It is Jesus Christ Who acts and forgives through His priests in the Sacrament of Penance.

Many stories of God's merciful love and forgiveness are recorded in the Bible; for example, Luke 7:36-48; Luke 15:11-24 and Matthew 9:2. The passage of John 20:19-23 relates how Jesus gave the Sacrament of Penance to the Church as His own Easter gift. After He had wished His Apostles peace, Our Lord said: "Receive the Holy Spirit; whose sins you shall forgive, they are forgiven them; and whose sins you shall retain, they are retained. "

Catholics should appreciate the wonderful Sacrament of Penance and receive it frequently. By their regular encounter with Jesus in sacramental Confession, they are privileged to hear Christ's words of forgiveness through the lips of His priest and receive God's pardon, peace, grace and love.

REVIEW QUESTIONS

1. What is Penance?

Penance is the sacrament by which Catholics receive God's merciful forgiveness for sins committed after Baptism. God's pardon is obtained through the sacramental absolution of a priest which is given when people are: sorry for their sins, resolve not to sin again and humbly confess their sins to a priest.

2. Should Catholics who are not guilty of serious sin receive the Sacrament of Penance?

Yes, Catholics who are not guilty of serious sin should receive the Sacrament of Penance frequently. This sacrament not only grants the forgiveness of sins but also gives an increase of grace which helps people break the habit of sin and advance in Christian perfection. It also provides an excellent opportunity to receive spiritual advice or direction from a priest.

3. If one has fallen into mortal sin, what is the ordinary way to obtain God's peace and forgiveness?

If one has fallen into mortal sin, the ordinary way to obtain God's peace and forgiveness is to receive the Sacrament of Penance worthily. The Bishops of the United States in *Basic Teachings for Catholic Religious Education* state: "If one has fallen into serious sin, sacramental Confession is the ordinary way established in the Church to reconcile the sinner with Christ and His Church."

4. When should children learn about the Sacrament of Penance and be taught how to go to Confession?

Children should learn about the Sacrament of Penance and be taught how to go to Confession at the same time they are being prepared for their first Holy Communion. This is the teaching of the Pope and the Bishops of the United States. The latter state: "...every Catholic, from his early years, should be

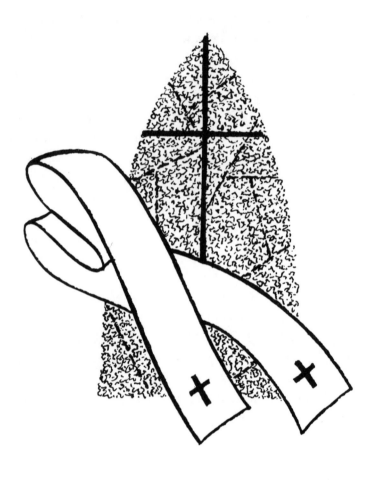

*Priests have the power to forgive sins
in the Sacrament of Penance.*

instructed how to receive and best profit from the regular reception of this sacrament' (Penance)." *Basic Teachings for Catholic Religious Education.*

DISCUSSION QUESTIONS

1. What effect does the Sacrament of Holy Orders have upon the souls of those who receive it?

2. What two special powers of Jesus do priests receive in the Sacrament of Holy Orders?

3. What does the Sacrament of Penance do for the soul?

4. What would you say to a person who stated that a priest cannot forgive sins because he is a man and no "mere man" can do this?

5. Does the Bible clearly state that Jesus gave His first priests, the Apostles, the power to forgive sins? Explain.

6. In order to receive the Sacrament of Penance worthily, what must one do in addition to confessing his sins to a priest?

7. Should Catholics go to Confession only when they are in the state of mortal sin? Explain.

8. What is meant by "frequent" Confession? Does the Church encourage this?

FOR OLDER STUDENTS

The sacrament of Penance is for the forgiveness of sins committed after Baptism and for healing of the soul. It is also called the sacrament of conversion, confession, penance, or reconciliation. It is the gift of the Father's mercy.

This is a special sacrament of the richness of the mercy of God. Jesus died on the cross to redeem us, to merit for us the forgiveness of sin. It is noteworthy then that the very first thing Jesus did after His crucifixion and death, when He faced His apostles after resurrection, was to give these first priests the power to forgive sin in His name. "He breathed on them, and said to them: 'Receive the Holy Spirit. If you forgive the sins of any, they are forgiven; if you retain the sins of any, they are retained.'" (Jn 20:19, 22-23).

One who has fallen into mortal sin can have confidence for salvation only by trusting in God's mercy. To desire God's forgiveness in His mercy is to have received the actual grace of conversion whereby one is moved to return to God. To desire to make a good confession and receive absolution from the priest is a response to actual grace whereby one desires to avoid evil and do good.

To be sincere in accepting this movement of the heart one must abhor the sins committed; have a firm purpose of sinning no more in the future. The person receiving these movements of the heart coming from God must be open to permit God to touch his heart as regard both the past and future. Three actions are required of the person seeking forgiveness in this sacrament. 1. Repentance. 2. Confession of all known mortal sins to an authorized Catholic priest. 3. Intend to make reparation for the sins committed. The penance the priest gives one at the time of confession is to help make reparation for sins committed.

The confession of all known mortal sins, after an examination of conscience, is required for a confession to be complete or integral. If one would deliberately not confess all his known mortal sins no sins would be forgiven even though some were confessed. That person would then be guilty of the mortal sin of sacrilege.

The confession of venial faults, while not necessary in itself, is strongly recommended by the Church for growth in virtue and grace of the sacrament.

The moment of forgiveness of sin in the sacrament of Penance is when the priest administers the sign of the sacrament, namely absolution with the words: "I absolve you from your sins in the name of the Father, and of the Son and of the Holy Spirit."

The effects of the sacrament of Penance are: reconciliation with God by recovering grace; reconciliation with the Church; remission of eternal punishment which one deserves while in mortal sin; remission of at least part of temporal punishment due to sin which would otherwise be endured in purgatory; peace of conscience and strength to fight sin in the future.

Catechism of the Catholic Church: 1420 - 1490.
Bible: 2 Cor 5:20; Mt 5:24; 1 Jn 1:8; Mk 1:15; Rev 2:5, 016;
    Jn 16:8-9; Lk 9:23; 15:11-24; Jn 20:21-23.

Questions to answer:

1. What is the significance of Jesus giving His Church the Sacrament of Penance for forgiveness of sin after His Resurrection?

2. What kind of grace is needed by one in mortal sin to repent and desire to make a good confession and what must the dispositions of heart be accompanying this desire?

3. A good confession must be integral with the confession

of all known mortal sins since one's last good confession. Why would God never forgive one mortal sin or some mortal sins without forgiving all mortal sins one had committed?

4. Explain what is meant by absolution in the sacrament of Penance.

●●●

POINTS FOR PARENTS AND TEACHERS

The Addendum of the General Catechetical Directory *issued by Rome and quoted by our American Bishops in* Basic Teachings for Catholic Religious Education *presents many important concepts about the Sacrament of Penance which should be understood and implemented by all Catholics, especially those who are instructing children in their faith. The following is significant:*

"The special task of catechesis here is to explain in a suitable way that sacramental Confession is a means offered children of the Church to obtain pardon for sin, and furthermore that it is even necessary per se *if one has fallen into serious sin. To be sure, Christian parents and religious educators ought to teach the child in such a way that above all he will strive to advance to a more intimate love of the Lord Jesus and to genuine love of neighbor. The doctrine on the Sacrament of Penance is to be presented in a broad framework of attaining purification and spiritual growth with great confidence in the mercy and love of God....One should also keep in mind the usefulness of Confession, which retains its efficacy even when only venial sins are in question, and which gives an increase of*

grace and of charity, increases the child's good dispositions for receiving the Eucharist, and also helps to perfect the Christian life."

Educators and parents should also know that on July 7, 1973, the Congregation for the Discipline of the Sacraments and the Congregation for the Clergy jointly issued a document ordering an end to experiments that permitted children to receive their first Communion before making their first Confession. This document, which was dated May 24, 1973, and had the approval of Pope Paul VI, stated:

"The Supreme Pontiff Pius X, in the decree, Quam Singulari *of August 8, 1910 (Acta Apostolicae Sedis, pp. 577-83), implementing the prescription of Canon XXI of the IV Lateran Council, ordered that children from the age of discretion might receive the Sacraments of Penance and Holy Eucharist. This precept, accepted into practice throughout the universal Church, brought, and continues to bring, much fruit for the Christian life and perfection of the spirit.*

"The Addendum of the General Catechetical Directory *promulgated by the Sacred Congregation for the Clergy on April 11, 1971 (Acta Apostolicae Sedis 1972, pp. 97-176), adds strength to the custom of administering the Sacrament of Penance before the first Communion of children with these words: 'Having weighed all these points, and keeping in mind the common and general practice which* per se *cannot be derogated without the approval of the Apostolic See, and also having heard the Conferences of Bishops, the Holy See judges it fitting that the practice now in force in the*

Church of putting Confession ahead of first Communion should be retained (No. 5).'

"... the Sacred Congregations for the Discipline of the Sacraments and for the Clergy, by this document, with the approval of the Supreme Pontiff Paul VI, declare that an end must be put to these experiments, which have extended over two years, with the conclusion of the current school year 1972-1973, and that the decree Quam Singulari is therefore to be henceforth obeyed everywhere and by all."

The Church has spoken clearly. Therefore, parents and educators should teach the Sacraments of Penance and Holy Eucharist SIMULTANEOUSLY so those preparing for first Holy Communion will know how to receive the Eucharist and sacramental absolution worthily. Furthermore, children must be given the opportunity to go to Confession before Holy Communion. All these considerations are merely "rights" of children that adults must respect. To neglect or deny Catholic youth in these matters is to tamper within the sanctuary of souls.

It should also be noted that parents and educators do NOT have the duty of deciding whether a child has to go to Confession before he receives first Holy Communion. Such matters are in the domain of the concerned individual's conscience. Although adults must never force children to receive the Sacrament of Penance, they may and should help and encourage them to do so.

Those who share in the religious instruction and guidance of youth have the serious obligation of teaching the Sacraments of Penance and Holy Eucharist and the reality of sin, which even children are capable of committing. However, they must do so in a POSITIVE way by emphasizing God's love and mercy and avoiding undue elements of fear. (It has been the experience of the *author of this book, a priest who has prepared first and second graders for the Sacraments of Penance and Holy Eucharist for 25 years and has heard the Confessions of those making their first Communion, that properly instructed children are eager to receive both sacraments.)*

In those areas where formal religious educational programs do not teach the Sacraments of Penance and Holy Eucharist simultaneously or where there are serious deficiencies in content or method, parents have the RIGHT and DUTY to prepare their children for Confession before first Holy Communion. They may also take their children to Confession to an understanding priest in any Parish Church because no permission is necessary for that which the highest authorities of the Church require.

Because there have been some unfortunate misconceptions about the Sacrament of Penance since the new rite for Confession was introduced in 1976, Catholics should understand that this rite still requires that penitents MUST have the option of going to Confession anonymously (through a screen) if they desire. Therefore, no one should be compelled to confess his sins openly in a Room of Reconciliation. Furthermore, general absolution of more than one penitent at a time without their previous individual Confession is not to be administered indiscriminately.

To summarize, the normal manner of receiving the Sacrament of Penance and Reconciliation is through private Confession and individual absolution of each penitent.

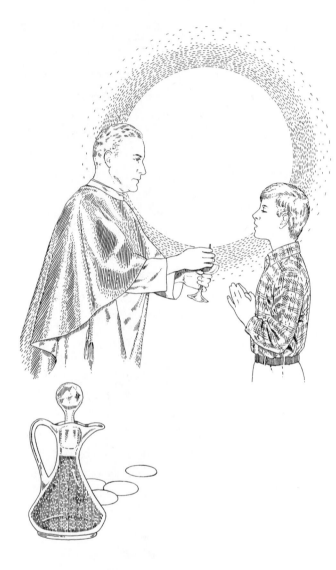

*Catholics receive the Body, Blood,
Soul and Divinity of Jesus Christ in the
Sacrament of the Holy Eucharist.*

The Holy Eucharist is, without doubt, the GREATEST of the seven sacraments which Christ instituted for His Church. This Sacrament of Love is Jesus Himself and is both a sacrifice and a sacrament.

As sacrifice, Our Lord perpetuates His death on the Cross in an unbloody manner at every Holy Mass. As sacrament, He gives men His BODY, BLOOD, SOUL and DIVINITY under the appearances of bread and wine in Holy Communion.

Although each of the seven sacraments is an ACTION and a SIGN of Christ, the Holy Eucharist is the only sacrament in which Our Lord is personally contained, offered and received.

Jesus Christ instituted the Holy Eucharist on Holy Thursday, the night before He died. Knowing He would sacrifice His life for mankind on Good Friday on Calvary, Jesus willed to continue to offer Himself for all time through His Church.

Every Holy Mass continues the action of the Last Supper and Calvary. At Holy Communion, when God the Father invites His people to eat of the acceptable gift offered to Him, the faithful are privileged to receive the Body, Blood, Soul and Divinity of Jesus Christ under the APPEARANCES of ordinary bread and wine.

Holy Mother the Church uses the word TRANSUB-STANTIATION to express the complete change of the entire substance of bread and wine into Christ's Body and Blood. (This takes place at the Consecration of the Holy Sacrifice of the Mass.) Transubstantiation means that Jesus Christ, true God and true Man, is really and substantially present in a mysterious but real way under the appearances of bread and wine after the priest says: "This is My Body...this is My Blood." Therefore, when Catholics receive Holy Communion, it is REALLY and TRULY Jesus Who comes into their souls.

Although the Holy Eucharist retains (keeps) the appearances (what a thing looks, tastes or feels like) of bread and wine after the Consecration, It is no longer bread and wine. Rather, the sacrament is then the LIVING and RISEN Christ because Its substance (what a thing actually is) has been changed by divine power.

Catholics should often thank God for His love and abiding presence in the Holy Eucharist. When Jesus, the Bread of Life, comes to souls in Holy Communion, He nourishes them with His own Flesh and Blood. That means each time Catholics receive Our Lord worthily, they share more abundantly in God's life (sanctifying grace). They also merit greater happiness in heaven and are assured that Christ will reunite their souls and resurrected bodies forever when He raises the bodies of all men from the grave at the end of the world.

Catholics should prayerfully read and study the entire Sixth Chapter of St. John. In this Gospel, Our Lord repeatedly states that He really comes to men in the Holy Eucharist, and He promises EVERLASTING LIFE to all who receive Him worthily. Yes, Jesus so loves and longs to be loved that He gives men nothing less than Himself in the Most Blessed Sacrament.

The Church teaches that Catholics must be in the STATE of GRACE to receive Jesus WORTHILY (I Corinthians 11:27). Therefore, those who go to Holy Communion knowing they are in the state of mortal sin do not receive God's graces and commit the grave sin of sacrilege.

It is only right that Catholics receive the Holy Eucharist with great faith, love, reverence and devotion. They should strive, as much as possible, to be free from venial sins. Although it is not necessary to go to Confession each time one goes to Communion, the Sacrament of Penance MUST be received before Holy Communion by persons guilty of mortal sin. Furthermore, frequent Confession is highly recommended for those who have committed only less serious sins because it brings an increase of grace and disposes the soul to receive Our Lord in Holy Communion more worthily.

Catholics should grow in their love for Jesus in the Blessed Sacrament and express this by internal and external acts of reverence and respect. For instance, when the priest elevates the CONSECRATED HOST and CHALICE at Holy Mass, they should look up, adore God and silently say an appropriate prayer, such as, "My Lord and my God." They should remember to genuflect when they enter and leave a Catholic Church and also each time they walk past the tabernacle. They may even wish to express their belief in the sacramental presence of Our Lord when they pass a Catholic Church by making a devout "Sign of the Cross" or saying a short prayer.

Because Benediction of the Blessed Sacrament, Holy Hours and other Eucharistic Devotions are fitting tributes to Our Eucharistic Lord, they should be attended with gratitude, fervor and love. Catholics should also strive to attend Holy

Mass daily, if possible, and make frequent visits to Our Lord in the Most Blessed Sacrament.

It is important that a good preparation and thanksgiving be made for Holy Communion. Catholics must take time to think about God and speak to Him both before and after He comes to them in the Holy Eucharist. They may do so by praying some of the approved prayers of the Church (such as acts of faith, hope, love, contrition, adoration, thanksgiving, reparation or petition, which can be found in a Catholic prayer book) or simply by talking to God in their own words.

Because Jesus remains sacramentally present within one after Holy Communion – so long as the sacred species retain their forms of bread and wine, i.e. until the digestive processes begin to change the form – Catholics should devote as much of this time as possible to personal prayer and intimate union with God.

Although men will never be able to understand fully the mystery of God's gift of Himself in the Most Holy Eucharist, they must try to do so. In this wonderful sacrament of unity, Jesus invites all men to be one with Him and each other. At the same time, He grants graces to those who receive Him and transforms them into His own image and likeness.

REVIEW QUESTIONS

1. What is the Holy Eucharist?

The Holy Eucharist is one of the seven sacraments instituted by Jesus Christ. It is both a sacrifice and a sacrament. As sacrifice, Jesus perpetuates His death on the Cross in every Holy Mass. As sacrament, He gives His Body, Blood, Soul and Divinity to the faithful in Holy Communion.

2. What word does the Church use to express the changing of bread and wine into the Body and Blood of Jesus Christ?

The Church uses the word "transubstantiation" to express the changing of bread and wine into the Body and Blood of Jesus Christ. (In a letter to the whole world, Pope Paul VI stated that "transubstantiation" is the proper word to use. Our American Bishops have said the same.)

"Trans" means "across" and "substantiation" means "substance" or that which a thing really is. "Transubstantiation" means that the substance of bread and wine is no longer present after the priest pronounces the words of Eucharistic Consecration: "This is My Body...this is My Blood." It means that Jesus Christ, true God and true Man, is Himself really and substantially present in a mysterious but real way under the "appearances" of bread and wine.

3. Does any of the substance of bread and wine remain after the words of Consecration?

No, absolutely none of the substance of bread and wine remains after the words of Consecration. It is only the "appearances" of bread and wine that remain. Therefore, the bread and wine still look, feel, taste and smell like bread and wine; but they are no longer bread and wine because their substance has been changed. It is really and truly the living Jesus Christ

Who is now present in the Holy Eucharist. That is why Catholics adore the Blessed Sacrament; genuflect when they walk past the tabernacle; make visits to the Church and always act with proper respect and reverence while in the presence of the Eucharist.

4. Is it necessary for Catholics to be in the state of sanctifying grace to receive Jesus worthily in Holy Communion?

Yes, it is necessary for Catholics to be in the state of sanctifying grace to receive Jesus worthily in Holy Communion. Those who knowingly receive the Holy Eucharist with mortal sin on their souls commit the serious sin of sacrilege and do not receive the Lord's graces.

It is most important that Catholics approach the altar with faith, reverence and love. They should even try to be free from venial sin, as far as this is possible. Frequent reception of the Sacrament of Penance is encouraged by the Church because it increases grace and helps men receive the Eucharist more worthily.

DISCUSSION QUESTIONS

1. Whom do Catholics receive in Holy Communion?

2. Why is the Holy Eucharist called the "greatest" sacrament?

3. When did Jesus institute the Sacrament of the Holy Eucharist?

4. Why did Jesus institute the Sacrament of the Holy Eucharist?

5. When does the bread and wine become the Body, Blood, Soul and Divinity of Jesus Christ?

6. What effects does the worthy reception of Holy Communion have upon the soul?

7. Is it necessary to go to Confession each time one receives the Holy Eucharist? Explain.

8. Should Catholics who are not in the state of mortal sin receive the Sacrament of Penance? Explain.

9. What sin do Catholics commit when they go to Holy Communion knowing they are in the state of mortal sin?

10. What dispositions should Catholics have when they participate at Holy Mass? Why?

11. What should Catholics do and say at the Elevation of the Mass?

12. When should Catholics genuflect? Why?

13. How long does Our Lord remain sacramentally present in the soul after Holy Communion?

14. Why should Catholics make a good thanksgiving after they receive Holy Communion?

●●●

FOR OLDER STUDENTS

While we considered the Holy Eucharist as "Sacrifice" in Lesson 12, in this lesson we consider the Eucharist as "Sacrament". All the other sacraments given to the Church by Jesus Christ are oriented toward the Eucharist. The Catechism of the Catholic Church quotes the Second Vatican Council saying: "The Eucharist is `the source and summit of the

Christian life.' ... For in the blessed Eucharist is contained the whole spiritual good of the Church, namely Christ himself, our Pasch" (1324). The Eucharist is the highest cause for continued communion in the divine life, or grace, and maintaining in being the unity of the members of the Church. It is especially through the Sacrifice of the Mass and reception of Jesus Christ in the Eucharist that we grow in sanctifying grace.

The very heart of the celebration of the Eucharist is when the bread and wine, by the words of Christ spoken by an ordained priest and the invocation of the Holy Spirit, become Christ's Body and Blood. These solemn words, "This is my Body.... This is my Blood" are called the "consecration" of the Mass.

Jesus prepared the faith of people to believe that He would give His Body to eat and His Blood to drink in the sacrament of the Eucharist when he multiplied the loaves of bread and changed water into wine at the wedding at Cana. The message of these miracles of Jesus tell us that there will always be a superabundance of the unique bread of the Eucharist changed into the Body of Jesus and that the supply of Jesus' Body through the centuries will never diminish. Faith in Jesus able to change water into wine prepares for faith in Jesus who is able to change wine into His precious blood.

St. Matthew, St. Mark and St Luke, who wrote the three synoptic gospels, each give an account of Jesus instituting the Eucharist. St. John who wrote his gospel later gives a detailed account of Jesus' teaching in the synagogue of Capernaum. There Jesus calls Himself "the bread of life, come down from heaven". He was preparing people for the institution of the Eucharist. St. John does not repeat what the other evangelists had already written in their gospels but he does go into great detail (in John 6) of Jesus' promise of the Holy Eucharist.

Jesus Christ is present in many ways to His Church. Jesus is present in His Word, namely the scriptures read in Church, in prayer, in the poor, the sick, the imprisoned. But Jesus is present most especially in the Eucharistic species. This sacramental presence of Jesus Christ, called the "Real Presence," is unique.

The Council of Trent, reaffirmed by the Second Vatican Council and quoted in the Catechism of the Catholic Church says that in the most blessed sacrament of the Eucharist "the body and blood, together with the soul and divinity, of our Lord Jesus Christ and, therefore, the whole Christ is truly, really and substantially contained" (1374).

The presence of Jesus Christ in the Eucharist is a presence in the fullest sense. It is a substantial living presence of Jesus Christ, true God and man, who therein makes Himself wholly and entirely present. The whole substance of the bread is changed into the substance of the body of Christ our Lord. The whole substance of the wine is changed into the substance of His blood. This change the holy Catholic Church calls transubstantiation.It is at the moment of the consecration that the Eucharistic presence of Jesus Christ begins. Jesus remains really present as long as the Eucharistic species of bread and wine remain after consecration. Christ is present whole and entire in each part of the Eucharistic bread or consecrated wine. Breaking of the eucharistic bread does not divide Christ. Whether a drop or larger portion of the wine consecrated into Jesus' blood is received, one receives the Jesus Christ whole and entire.

Jesus Christ is worshipped in the Eucharist not only during Mass but outside of Mass. Benediction of the Blessed Sacrament and carrying the Eucharist in reverent procession are encouraged. The faithful are encouraged to visit Jesus in the Blessed Sacrament in gratitude for His presence in our midst and for His love for us and to offer Him adoration.

The Eucharist is reserved in the tabernacle for our adoration and also that the sacrament is available to be taken to the sick. When reserved in the tabernacle this Sacrament is often called "the most Blessed Sacrament." The tabernacle, says the universal Catechism, should be located in "an especially worthy place in the church and should be constructed in such a way that it emphasizes and manifests the truth of the real presence of Christ in the Blessed Sacrament." The Church encourages silent adoration of our Lord present under the Eucharistic species. One should genuflect upon entering a Church or chapel where the Blessed Sacrament is reserved and genuflect whenever passing in front of this Sacrament.

When the Eucharist is received it is known as Holy Communion. One must be free of mortal sin, that is, in the state of sanctifying grace to worthily receive our Lord in Holy Communion. One must observe the fast required before reception of this sacrament. Gestures and clothing should reflect the solemnity of receiving Jesus Christ in Holy Communion with deep reverence and respect after which a fitting thanksgiving should be made.

Since Jesus is present in every particle of either species of the Eucharist, Holy Communion received under the species of bread alone makes possible all the grace this sacrament offers. This practice is established in the Latin rite as the most common form. The sign is more complete under both species but not the spiritual fruit of the sacrament.

While the ideal is to receive Holy Communion at every Mass, even daily, if one is in the state of grace, Church Law requires the Eucharist at least once a year, especially during the

Easter season. Holy Communion increase one's union with our Lord, forgives venial sins, preserves one more strongly from the dangers to mortal sin; strengthens the bonds of charity between the communicant and Jesus Christ while also strengthening the bond of unity of the members of the Mystical Body of Christ.

Catechism of the Catholic Church: 1322-1419.
Bible: 1 Cor 10:16; Mt 14:13-21; 15:32-39; Jn 2:11; Jn 6;
   Lk 22:7-20; Mt 26:17-29; Mk 14:25; Jn 6:60, 67, 68;
   13:1-17; 34-35. 1 Cor 11:26; Acts 2:42, 46, 20:7.

Questions to answer:

1. Explain how each of the following sacraments are oriented toward the Holy Eucharist: Baptism, Penance, Confirmation, Holy Orders.

2. Receiving the Holy Eucharist as "Viaticum" when in danger of death along with the Anointing of the Sick is dealt with in chapter 21. At this time explain as best you can how this Anointing sacrament is also oriented to the Holy Eucharist.

3. Could a Catholic married couple live a state of Matrimony that was holy without the frequent and worthy reception of Holy Communion?

4. How are the miracles of Jesus multiplying loaves of bread and changing water into wine associated with the Holy Eucharist?

5. Is the real presence of Jesus Christ in the sacrament of the Holy Eucharist the same as His presence in the Word of

God read in Church? Explain answer.

6. What is necessary to receive our divine Lord worthily in Holy Communion?

●●●

POINTS FOR PARENTS AND TEACHERS

The Church has declared that the Holy Eucharist has primacy among the sacraments. Therefore, young Catholics should be well informed about this sacrament. Avoiding all scrupulosity, they must take to heart the message contained in I Cor. 11:27 which the Bishops have restated: namely, one must be in the state of grace to receive the Eucharist worthily.

They should also cultivate a profound sense of adoration for the Real Presence of the God-Man in the Holy Eucharist and be taught to make a good thanksgiving after Holy Communion, prolonging this, if possible, after Mass is completed.

Unfortunately, there are some modern Eucharistic celebrations where aberrations are in effect. Such liturgies do much to destroy the faith, reverence and sense of adoration which Catholics should have towards the Holy Eucharist as a sacrifice and sacrament.

Lesson 12 considered the Holy Eucharist as SACRIFICE. This lesson emphasizes it as SACRAMENT. Educators should frequently review the aspects of the Holy Eucharist as SACRIFICE so young Catholics truly understand that every Holy Mass is a perpetuation of the Sacrifice of the Cross. They should also realize that each time they assist at Holy Mass, they participate in Jesus' offering on Calvary. (A picture of people kneeling before an altar with a priest presiding at Mass next to an illustration of people

*gathered around Our Lord on the Cross may help students under-
stand that the SAME sacrifice is offered at Mass and Calvary.
Only the "MANNER of offering" is different.)*

Vatican Council II reminded Catholics that Jesus is present
when Sacred Scripture is read, especially during liturgical celebrations. Jesus is also present in the Community of the Faithful (the
Mystical Body) and in the Most Blessed Sacrament.

Unfortunately, some people have taught the presence of Jesus
in these three contexts: the Word, the People of God, and the Holy
Eucharist— as if all three were one and the same or as if Jesus
were present in the same manner in each. Such is not the case.

Surely it is necessary that Catholics acknowledge the importance
of Christ's presence when two or more are gathered together in His
Name. Likewise, they must recognize the communication of Jesus
through His Word in Scripture, particularly in the first part of the
Mass called the "Liturgy of the Word." At the same time, they must
NOT play down the Real Substantial Presence of the God-Man,
Jesus Christ, in His Body, Blood, Soul and Divinity.

Because the REAL PRESENCE of Jesus in the Blessed
Sacrament is not merely a spiritual presence, it cannot be equated
with Christ's presence in His Word or His presence in the members
of His Mystical Body, the Church. The Sacrifice of the Cross perpetuated and the Real Sacramental Presence of Jesus are, indeed,
the central mysteries of our holy Catholic Faith and worship.
Therefore, when parents and educators teach about the three different kinds of presence of Christ, they must avoid the extreme and
never lead youth to regard the Word of God in Scripture as equal
to or the same as the Presence of Jesus Christ sacramentally living
in the Blessed Sacrament.

Although Christ is truly present in different ways under different aspects, His REAL PRESENCE in the SACRAMENT OF
THE ALTAR is unique. ONLY in the Holy Eucharist is He pre-

sent in His BODY, BLOOD, SOUL and DIVINITY. Jesus remains sacramentally with His people through the action of the Sacrifice of the Mass and is both adored and received in the Most Holy Eucharist.

The Mystical Body, the Church, is most fully realized when it is gathered together with its bishop at Holy Mass. The Sacrifice of the Mass is truly a sacred meal in the community aspect, but it should never be regarded in a merely "natural" way because it is a SACRED BANQUET prepared for God's people.

Therefore, young Catholics must not think of the Sacrifice of the Mass simply as a Christian community at meal. Rather, they must understand that at every Holy Mass, the members of Christ become one with Jesus the High Priest as He perpetuates His Sacrifice on the Cross.

Filled with reverence and appreciation for the Holy Sacrifice of the Mass, Catholics should strive to participate attentively and completely at Holy Mass by worthily eating and drinking the Body and Blood of the Lord while they remain mindful of Christ's promise of resurrection and eternal life.

The Holy Eucharist is the GREATEST
sacrament instituted by Jesus Christ
for the Church. This sacrament is Jesus
Himself, and is both a sacrifice
and a sacrament.

LESSON 20
THE APOSTOLIC CHAIN:
HOLY ORDERS

Our Lord personally chose and taught the twelve Apostles, who were the first bishops and priests of His Church. When Jesus ordained the Apostles, they received the FULL-NESS of His holy priesthood and clearly understood they had the POWER to give this sacrament to others. Today the direct and full successors of Jesus' Apostles are the bishops, whom the Church calls the "College of Bishops." Only they have the power to ordain other men priests or bishops.

Holy Orders is sometimes called the Sacrament of the Priesthood. In this ONE sacrament, there are three major and separate orders: deacon, priest and bishop. Men who receive any of the orders of priesthood are marked with a special indelible character of Christ on their souls and are conformed to Jesus the High Priest, Who is the Mediator between God and man.

Although all deacons, priests and bishops possess SPECIAL POWERS of Christ's priesthood which other baptized and con-firmed Catholics do not have, there is a difference in the DEGREE of participation in Jesus' priestly powers for those ordained to the three major orders. As men progress through the stages or levels in Holy Orders, from deacon to priest or from priest to bishop, they become more fully identified with Christ and thus receive a greater share in His priestly powers.

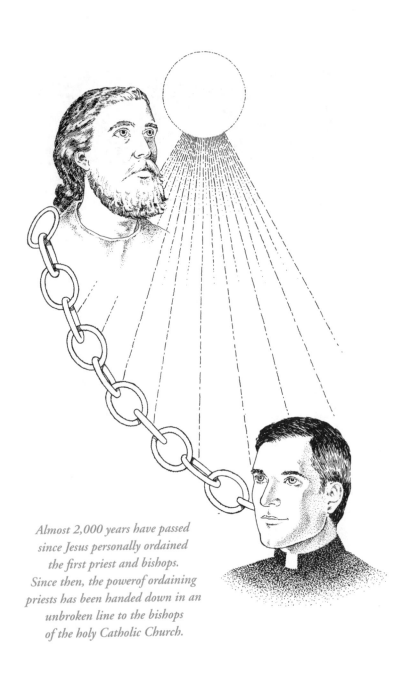

*Almost 2,000 years have passed
since Jesus personally ordained
the first priest and bishops.
Since then, the power of ordaining
priests has been handed down in an
unbroken line to the bishops
of the holy Catholic Church.*

Men ordained to the FIRST order of the Sacrament of the Priesthood are called DEACONS. This order dates back to the days of the Apostles. In fact, the very first martyr of the Church was a deacon named Stephen. Deacons are frequently mentioned in the Bible, particularly in that part called the "Acts of the Apostles." (Acts 6:5, I Tim. 3:1-13).

To some degree, deacons possess the indelible character of Jesus on their souls. They have the right to perform certain ministries in the Church such as: teaching, helping with the distribution of Holy Communion, baptizing, performing marriage ceremonies, etc. However, deacons CANNOT change bread and wine into the Body and Blood of Jesus, forgive sins or anoint the sick because these supernatural powers are given ONLY to men ordained to the order of priest or bishop.

Because there is a shortage of priests in some areas of the world today, the Church has approved that certain persons be appointed "extraordinary ministers of the Eucharist. " Although these people are NOT "ordained deacons," they have the privilege of helping priests distribute Holy Communion. The present need for extraordinary ministers of the Eucharist should prompt Catholics to pray and work for priestly vocations. It should also remind young Catholic boys to follow Our Lord, if He is calling them to this way of life.

Most Christians are familiar with the second major order of the priesthood because priests have given outstanding witness for Christ and served His Church for centuries.

When men are ordained PRIESTS, their souls are stamped with the indelible mark of Jesus and they are made "priests forever." The Sacrament of Holy Orders bestows upon them the supernatural powers to change ordinary bread and wine into the Body and Blood of Jesus in the Holy Sacrifice of the Mass and to forgive sins in the Sacrament of Penance. It also enables them to anoint the sick, preach with authority, bless people and things and administer all the sacraments of the Church except Holy Orders. (Although the bishop is the usual minister of Confirmation, priests can give this sacrament to those who seriously need it.) As they follow Christ, their Master and Teacher, and share in His ministry, priests serve, heal, strengthen and guide God's holy people, the Church.

Priests noted for their learning and holiness are chosen by the Holy Father, the Pope, to be consecrated BISHOPS. Possessing the fullness of the Sacrament of Christ's Priesthood, bishops are appointed as heads of dioceses. (A diocese is a specific part of God's Church. It usually is made up of many parishes.) All priests and Catholics must respect and obey their bishop because he, under the Pope and in union with him, has the chief spiritual authority in his diocese. Because bishops are the true successors to the Apostles, they have the special POWER to confirm, ordain and consecrate.

Almost 2,000 years have passed since Jesus personally ordained the first priests and bishops. Since then, the power of ordaining priests has been handed down in an unbroken line to the bishops of the holy Catholic Church. The term "apostolic chain" refers to this direct, unbroken line that connects the first Apostles to the present bishops of the Church. It means that every Catholic bishop today is a living link in a continuous chain of validly ordained bishops who have passed on the powers of Holy Orders through the twenty centuries of Church history. Therefore, only men ordained by a true bishop on the apostolic chain have the powers of the Sacrament of Holy Orders which Jesus gave to the Apostles.

Men who have received the Sacrament of Holy Orders

should be respected because they have been called to a sublime vocation. In particular, priests and bishops deserve special honor, reverence and appreciation since they alone have the power to forgive sins and offer the Church's greatest prayer, the Holy Sacrifice of the Mass.

Catholics must sincerely thank God for the blessings they receive through priests and remember to pray for them. Above all, they should realize that the respect, obedience, service, support and filial love given to priests is given to Christ—for priests are, in truth, "other Christs."

Priests are "other Christs" who have received through the Sacrament of Holy Orders the power of God to forgive sins, to change bread and wine into the Body and Blood of Jesus, to teach in Christ's name and to administer other sacraments of the Church.

REVIEW QUESTIONS

1. What is the Sacrament of Holy Orders?

Holy Orders is one of the seven sacraments instituted by Jesus Christ. By it, certain members of the Church are conformed to the High Priest, Jesus Christ, Who is the Mediator between God and man.

Holy Orders imparts a special indelible mark of Christ on the soul and gives men special powers of Jesus which other baptized and confirmed members of the Church do not have.

The Sacrament of Holy Orders is sometimes referred to as the Sacrament of the Priesthood. It consists of three separate, major orders: deacon, priest and bishop.

2. Why is the Sacrament of the Priesthood called "Holy Orders"?

The Sacrament of the Priesthood is called Holy Orders because it gives men the powers of Christ's priesthood which they receive in different degrees as they are ordained deacon, priest or bishop. As men progress through the three levels in the Sacrament of Holy Orders (from deacon to priest or from priest to bishop), they become more fully identified with Christ and receive a greater share in His priestly powers.

A Catholic priest has the chief powers of changing bread and wine into the Body, Blood, Soul and Divinity of Jesus Christ in the Holy Sacrifice of the Mass and of forgiving sins in the Sacrament of Penance. He also has power to preach with authority, to anoint the sick, to bless people and things and to administer all the sacraments of the Church except Holy Orders. (Although the bishop is the usual minister of Confirmation, the priest can give this sacrament to those who seriously need it.)

A deacon has the right to perform many special ministries in the Church such as: teaching, helping with the distribution of Holy Communion, baptizing, performing marriage ceremonies, etc.

3. Is it ONLY a difference of "degree" in which God's people share in Christ's priesthood through the Sacraments of Baptism, Confirmation and Holy Orders?

No, it is not only a difference of DEGREE in which God's people share in Christ's priesthood through the Sacraments of Baptism, Confirmation and Holy Orders; it is also a difference in ESSENCE.

This means that men who have received the Sacrament of Holy Orders have special powers for building up Christ's Mystical Body which other baptized and confirmed members of the Church do not possess.

The Bishops state that "Through this sacrament (Holy Orders) Christ bestows a permanent charism of the Holy Spirit...(that enables those who receive it) to guide and shepherd the faith community, proclaim and explain the Gospel, and guide and sanctify God's people."

4. What is meant by "apostolic chain"?

The "apostolic chain" refers to the unbroken line of apostolic succession in the holy Catholic Church whereby the powers of the priesthood, which were given to the first bishops of the Church (the Apostles), have been handed down to the bishops of the Catholic Church today.

Because every Catholic bishop in the world today was ordained by another validly ordained bishop, and he by another, each links on to other bishops in an unbroken chain through the twenty centuries of Church history. Thus, the chain of apostolic succession, which started with the Apostles whom Jesus Christ ordained, has been continued right to the present time. Therefore, a man must be ordained by a true bishop on the apostolic chain if he is to receive the powers of priesthood or Holy Orders which Jesus gave to His first priests, the Apostles.

DISCUSSION QUESTIONS

1. What special powers do Catholic priests receive when they are ordained?

2. Do baptized and confirmed Catholics have the same powers as Catholic priests? Explain.

3. Who is the Chief Priest Who shares His powers with Catholic priests?

4. What are the three major orders in the Sacrament of Holy Orders? Explain the duties and powers of each order.

5. Will the indelible character imprinted on a priest's soul at ordination remain in eternity? Explain.

6. Who is the only person who can truly ordain or give the Sacrament of Holy Orders?

7. What is meant by "apostolic chain"?

FOR OLDER STUDENTS

Holy Orders is the sacrament through which the mission entrusted to the apostles by Jesus Christ continues to be exercised by men in the Church until the end of time in apostolic succession. A bishop is given the fullness of the priesthood of Jesus Christ as given to the Apostles who were taught, formed and ordained by Jesus Christ Himself. Jesus continues to act through the bishops. One ordained is able to act as Christ's representative in the role as priest, prophet, and king.

There are three degrees to Holy Orders: bishops, presbyters, and deacons.

The Catechism of the Catholic Church, quoting the Second Vatican Council's Dogmatic Constitution on the Church explains apostolic succession this way: "Since the sacrament of Holy Orders is the sacrament of the apostolic ministry, it is for the bishops as the successors of the apostles to hand on the 'gift of the Spirit,' the 'apostolic line.' Validly ordained bishops, i.e., those who are in the line of apostolic succession, validly confer the three degrees of the sacrament of Holy Orders."

The sacrament of the priesthood confers a gift of the Holy Spirit which bestows a sacred power which can come only from Jesus Christ Himself through His Church. It is not then a mere election of the community but the call of Jesus Christ Himself speaking through His Church and acting through His bishops.

The sign of this sacrament is the laying on of hands by the bishop, with a special prayer of consecration. The man validly ordained receives a special indelible character or seal of Jesus Christ which is imprinted for ever on his soul. The vocation given at ordination marks the man permanently.

The whole Church of baptized believers form a priestly people, known as the "common priesthood". The priesthood conferred by Holy Orders is a ministerial priesthood which differs in essence from the common priesthood of the faithful because it confers a sacred power for service of the faithful and special power to give adoration to God, especially through the Eucharist. The ministerial priesthood exercises teaching authority in Jesus Christ's name, divine worship in the person of Jesus Christ, and pastoral governance for the good of souls. The ministerial priesthood of Holy Orders is essential for the existence of the nature of the Church. The Church can exist and do its work only with the bishop, priests, and deacons. The bishop receives the fullness of the sacrament of Holy Orders which makes him a member of the college of bishops and visible head of a particular local Church, (diocese) entrusted to him. Bishops as successors of the apostles share in the apostolic mission of the entire Church under the authority of the Pope, who is the successor of St. Peter. Only the Bishop can ordain priests and deacons.

A man consecrated a bishop receives the office of sanctifying, teaching and ruling. The grace of the Holy Spirit is received and a sacred character is impressed on the soul so that bishops in a special and visible manner, take the place of Jesus Christ as teacher, shepherd and priest.

A man may be lawfully ordained a bishop, by another

bishop, only by the intervention and designation of the Bishop of Rome, the Supreme Pontiff, since the Pope is the supreme visible bond of unity of particular local churches throughout the world with the one Church established by Jesus Christ.

The apostles chosen and ordained by Jesus Christ, whom the Father had sent into the world, were ordained bishops making them sharers in Christ's consecration and mission to the world. The first bishops in turn entrusted in varying degrees various members of the Church with the office of their ministry. The bishop's ministry was thus handed over in a subordinate degree to priests so that one ordained to the order of priesthood could be a co-worker of the episcopal order for the fulfillment of the apostolic mission entrusted the apostles by Jesus Christ.

Priests depend on the bishops in the exercise of their priestly power and are associated with the bishop in priestly dignity. Priests are thus ordained by the bishop to preach the Gospel, shepherd the faithful and celebrate the divine and eucharistic worship. In the Eucharistic worship priests exercise in a supreme degree their sacred office, acting in the person of Jesus Christ and proclaiming his mystery. They thus make present the unique sacrifice of the New Testament, that is, Jesus Christ offering Himself as victim to God the Father.

Deacons receive the imposition of hands, according to the Second Vatican Council's Dogmatic Constitution on the Church, "not unto the priesthood, but unto ministry" (LG 29). Deacons also receive a permanent "character" on their souls from Holy Orders which cannot be removed and which configures them more unto Christ in the role of service in assisting bishops and priests.

The Church confers the sacrament of Holy Orders only on

baptized men (viri), and Pope John Paul II said it must be held definitively that only men, not women, may be ordained to the priesthood as Jesus Christ gave the Church the authority to ordain only men. The Church normally in the Latin rite requires that men called to the priesthood take the vow of celibacy, that is, not to marry.

Catechism of the Catholic Church: 1536 - 1600.
Bible: Acts 1:8; 2:4; Jn 20:22-23; 1 Tim 4:14; 2 Tim 1:6-; Titus 1:5-9; Heb 5:4; Eph 4:11.

Questions to answer:

1. What is the sign of the sacrament of Holy Orders and who may administer it?

2. Explain why it is totally false to suppose that the community could elect who should be priests or bishops?

3. Is there difference in degree of participation in the priesthood of Jesus Christ between priesthood of the baptized and the ministerial priesthood of Holy Orders? Explain answer.

4. What is the role of ordained deacons?

5. Could the true Church exist without the priesthood? Why?

●●●

POINTS FOR PARENTS AND TEACHERS

The following facts should be stressed when teaching the Sacrament of Holy Orders:

1. *The holy priesthood has a permanent nature.*
2. *The powers of the priest are not merely 'functional.' "**
3. *Holy Orders makes the priest a unique member of the Church.*
4. *Catholics should have a profound sense of respect for priests.*

The Catholic priest has powers no other man on earth possesses. Indeed, they are the powers of Jesus Christ in Whose special character his soul is sealed in the Sacrament of Holy Orders.

Although men who are not ordained by a bishop on the apostolic chain could perform the FUNCTIONS of a priest, the divine actions of Christ would NEVER take place. For this reason, the Catholic Church does not recognize the ordained powers of Christ in Protestant ministers, but it does acknowledge the valid priesthood and Eucharist of some Orthodox churches.

---

*Martin Luther and others who broke away from the true Church stated that all baptized Christians had EQUAL powers, and that those who functioned as priests had no special spiritual powers. Such belief is contrary to Catholic teaching.

LESSON 21
THE ANOINTING
OF THE SICK

God has a special love and compassion for the sick and infirm. When Our Lord lived on earth, He often cured people by merely speaking a word. Today Jesus continues to show His mercy and concern for those who suffer physically. He does this in a special way through the Sacrament of the Anointing of the Sick.

This sacrament, instituted by Christ for the seriously ill, infirm and aged, is mentioned in the Bible. St. James described it when he wrote what must be done for someone gravely ill. He said, "...bring in the presbyters of the Church, and let them pray over him, anointing him with oil in the name of the Lord" (James 5:14).

This is precisely what a Catholic priest does when he administers the Sacrament of the Anointing of the Sick. He anoints the person in need with special oil, which has been consecrated by the bishop on Holy Thursday at the Cathedral Church, and prays for God's help and forgiveness. In this sacrament, Jesus Christ personally acts, touching the soul with His POWER.

Oil is a SIGN of healing and strength. The Anointing of the Sick always strengthens the soul.

Sometimes it heals the body, when this is for the good of the soul.

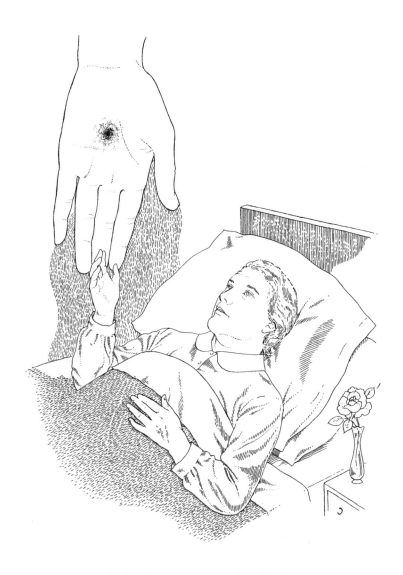

Today, Jesus continues to show His love,
mercy and compassion for the sick
and infirm. He does this in a special way
through the Sacrament of the Anointing
of the Sick.

A person only has to be in DANGER of death to receive the Sacrament of the Anointing. Therefore, it is not correct to call this sacrament the " Sacrament of the Dying. " Because the sacrament is BEST received as soon as the danger of death BEGINS, Catholics should immediately call a priest when any one who is old, infirm, injured or seriously ill is in danger of death.

The Sacrament of the Anointing has many effects. It gives a special supernatural value to suffering and enables the sick and dying to unite their sufferings with Jesus' sufferings and to accept their illness, pain or death as God's will. This sacrament also brings an increase of sanctifying grace and confidence in God, strengthens souls to resist temptation and prepares them for heaven.

The Sacrament of the Anointing of the Sick takes away all VENIAL SINS and at least SOME, if not all, of the temporal punishment due to sin. However, all conscious and able Catholics who are aware of being in the state of mortal sin MUST go to Confession before they are anointed. For persons unconscious or unable to receive the Sacrament of Penance, the Anointing of the Sick takes away even serious sins PRO-VIDED these persons were in SOME WAY sorry for their sins BEFORE they became unconscious or disabled.

Catholics should always call a priest to attend a person who has died a sudden or unexpected death. The priest will pray for the dead person and may give "conditional" absolution and anointing.

When Catholics properly understand the Anointing of the Sick, they are neither frightened by this sacrament nor hesitant to call a priest when someone is seriously ill or in danger of death. Recognizing Jesus in this sacrament, they are comforted, consoled and encouraged, for they know His ACTION, POWER and PRESENCE bring all that is needed for eternal happiness and union with God.

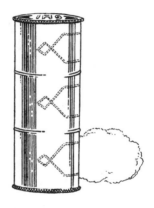

". .. bring in the presbyters of the Church,
and let them pray over him, anointing him
with oil in the name of the Lord. "
—James 5:14

REVIEW QUESTIONS

1. What is the Sacrament of the Anointing of the Sick?

The Anointing of the Sick is the sacrament for the seriously ill, infirm and aged. It is best received as soon as the danger of death (from either accident, sickness or old age) begins.

2. What are the effects of the Sacrament of the Anointing of the Sick?

The Sacrament of the Anointing of the Sick has many effects:

It gives an increase of sanctifying grace.

It enables the sick or dying person to accept with supernatural power the will of Christ in his sickness or death.

It prepares the soul for its entrance into eternity.

It unites (and thus sanctifies) the suffering of the anointed to the sufferings and death of Jesus.

It comforts the soul and strengthens it to resist temptation.

It strengthens one's confidence in God's mercy and love.

It takes away venial sin and some, if not all, of the temporal punishment due to sin.

Sometimes it restores bodily health.

This sacrament can also take away mortal sin if a person is unconscious and unable to confess his sins, providing he was in some way sorry for his sins before he became unconscious.

3. Is the Anointing of the Sick only for persons who are dying?

No, the Anointing of the Sick is not only for persons who are dying; it is also for those who are seriously ill. When Holy Communion is received by a dying person, it is called VIATICUM. The anointing is for all who have attained the use of reason and are seriously ill. It should be received as soon as the danger of death is present.

4. Should a priest be called to attend a person who has died suddenly?

Yes, a priest should be called to attend a person who has died suddenly. He will pray for the person, asking God to forgive him his sins and receive his soul into heaven. The priest may also CONDITIONALLY absolve and anoint the person.

DISCUSSION QUESTIONS

1. Who should receive the Sacrament of the Anointing of the Sick?

2. When is the Sacrament of the Anointing of the Sick best received?

3. Why is the name "Sacrament of the Anointing of the Sick" used rather than the "Sacrament of the Dying"?

4. Which members of the Church have the power to administer the Sacrament of the Anointing of the Sick?

5. What does the Sacrament of the Anointing do for sick persons?

6. How does the Sacrament of the Anointing help a person suffer "supernaturally"?

7. Does the Sacrament of the Anointing of the Sick ever take away mortal sin? Explain.

8. Would a person who was conscious and able to confess his sins need to go to Confession before receiving the Sacrament of the Anointing if his conscience told him he was in the state of mortal sin? Explain.

9. Should a priest be called to anoint a person who has died a sudden death? Why?

FOR OLDER STUDENTS

The Bible speaks clearly of the sacrament of the sick through St. James the Apostle. The sick are thus commended to the suffering and glorified Lord, and they are exhorted to unite themselves to the Passion and death of Christ.

Only priests and bishops have the power of Jesus Christ to give the sacrament of the Anointing of the Sick. The sign of this sacrament, together with the words, is the anointing with oil blessed by the bishop. The priest after laying his hands on the sick, praying over them in the faith of the Church, anoints the forehead, saying: "Through this holy anointing may the Lord in his love and mercy help you with the grace of the Holy Spirit." R. Amen. Then he anoints the hands, saying: "May the Lord who frees you from sin save you and raise you up." R. Amen.

The Church received from Jesus the command "Heal the sick!" (Mt 10:8). Jesus's compassion toward sick and suffering people is evident in the Bible. He often healed every kind of infirmity. Jesus while physically on earth not only healed but forgave sins. Jesus even identified with the sick: "I was sick and you visited me" (Mt 25:36).

The Holy Spirit sometimes gives to certain persons a special charism for healing when it is the will of God that a healing take place. One may receive this sacrament each time he falls seriously ill. It may be received a second time during the same illness if the illness grows more serious.

When the one to be anointed has the use of his mental faculties and is able to confess, he must receive the Sacrament of Reconciliation first, if his conscience accuses him of mortal sin. The sacrament does have the power to remove sin if a person is unable to confess and had proper dispositions of heart previously. The sacrament may be given in the family home, hospital or the church. The ideal time to receive it is within the celebration of the Eucharist, the memorial of the Lord's Passover. At times parishes may administer the sacrament in the context of the Sacrifice of the Mass to a group of persons who are deserving because of old age or other reasons but are still able to come to the Church.

In addition to the Anointing of the Sick, when persons are about to leave this life, they receive our Lord in Holy Communion which is then called "Viaticum" (With you on your way). The Body and Blood, Soul and Divinity of Jesus Christ thus received is the seed of eternal life with the power of future resurrection. At such a time the Eucharist is the sacrament of passing over from death to life, from this world to God the Father.

In danger of death the priest may also give the Apostolic Pardon for the dying which asks almighty God to release the person from all punishments in this life and in the life to come. This Apostolic Blessing brings with it a plenary indulgence.

Catechism of the Catholic Church: 1499 - 1532.
Bible: Jas 5:14-16; Rom 8:17; Col 1:24; 2 Tim 2:11-12; 1 Pet 4:13; Lk 7:16; Mt 4:24; 25:36; 8:17; Mk 2:5-12; 2:17; 6:16:17-18; Jn 1:29; 6:54: 13:1).

Questions to answer:

1. Who in the Church has the power of Jesus Christ to administer the sacrament of the Anointing of the Sick?

2. How did Jesus react toward the sick while He was physically upon earth during His earthly ministry?

3. What effects does the Anointing have on the souls of sick persons? What effects sometimes on the body?

4. Why is the Eucharist called "Viaticum" when administered in danger of death?

5. What is the meaning and effect of the Apostolic Pardon?

●●●

POINTS FOR PARENTS AND TEACHERS

The Sacrament of the Anointing of the Sick must be properly presented to young Catholics. They must realize this sacrament is not meant exclusively for the dying. The Church emphasizes "Anointing of the Sick" rather than "Extreme Unction" to prevent this misunderstanding. In the past, some have mistakenly thought "Extreme Unction" was only for this purpose.

Catholics are anointed several times during their lives—first at Baptism and again at Confirmation. Men who receive the Sacrament of Holy Orders are also anointed. The Anointing of the Sick usually takes place when one is seriously ill or in danger of death.

A point that merits emphasis and repetition is that special supernatural value is given to natural suffering by the Anointing of the Sick. Therefore, when this sacrament is delayed unnecessarily, Catholics with prolonged illnesses are deprived of having their sufferings sacramentalized and joined to Jesus' sufferings through the special sacrament He gave the Church for this purpose.

It is essential that young people understand that Christ is the Chief Priest of every sacrament. (Vatican II stressed this fact.) Therefore, each time a Catholic receives a sacrament, he has a personal encounter with Christ, for it is really He Who baptizes, confirms, anoints the sick, etc.

God instituted marriage and blessed it from the beginning of time. He created Adam and Eve, our first parents, as adults and made them for each other as husband and wife. God intended that their marriage be a model for all marriages. Therefore, He created only ONE wife for Adam. Furthermore, He instructed them to have children and share in His own power of creation and love when He said, "...'Be fruitful and multiply; fill the earth...' " (Genesis 1:28).

Unfortunately, all men did not follow God's laws and plan. The Bible tells of many husbands, wives, men and women who robbed marriage of its purpose, beauty and sacredness by their sinful, selfish lives.

However, in time, the holiness of marriage was restored when the world was given a new model for family life. This happened when Jesus Christ, the Second Person of the Blessed Trinity, became Man and chose to be born as a helpless baby into a real family. Later, during his adult public life, Jesus openly condemned those who refused to use marriage according to God's laws. Moreover, before He died, Jesus raised the dignity of marriage by making it one of the seven sacraments of the Church.

When Joseph and Mary were married, they truly became husband and wife. With Jesus, they formed the Holy Family.

*Catholic homes, as miniature churches,
should reflect the holiness, love, obedience
and joy of the Holy Family.*

The Blessed Virgin Mary, as the real physical mother of Jesus, became a shining model for all Christian wives and mothers. Her virginal spouse, St. Joseph, fulfilled the duties of his vocation so faithfully that he now serves as the outstanding example for Christian husbands and fathers. Jesus Christ, the God-Man, was a perfect Son and lived in complete subjection to His parents. Children of all ages should pattern their childhood and entire lives after His.

Although all baptized persons are united as one in Christ's Church, marriage joins two baptized Christians together in Jesus in a special way until death. Jesus Himself clearly said that those who are married remain married until one of the spouses dies. This law of God, which is plainly stated in many parts of the Bible (I Corinthians 7:10-11 and 39, Mark 10:6-12, Romans 7:2-3), can never be changed by any man-made law or court ruling. Because men and women are not free to change their minds about being husband and wife once they are truly married, those who are married and those who are thinking about getting married must understand that marriage lasts until death.

Church law states that Catholics should marry Catholics. Mixed marriages (marriages in which one of the partners is Catholic and the other non-Catholic) are discouraged "in order to encourage a full union of mind and life in matrimony." (These are the precise words of the American Bishops.) Any Catholic who wishes to marry a person of another faith must have a serious reason for doing so and then obtain special permission from his bishop before he can receive the Sacrament of Matrimony. Furthermore, Catholics who enter mixed marriages must promise to have all their children baptized and reared as Catholics because they are bound to do all in their power to share their true faith.

The proper place for all Catholics to be married is in a Catholic Church before an authorized Catholic priest. This holds true for mixed marriages, too. Therefore, Catholics who "attempt" marriage outside the Catholic Church without an authorized Catholic priest as the chief witness and without a dispensation from the bishop are entering a sinful state. The Church does NOT consider such persons lawfully married in the mind of God.

Those planning to marry must be aware of the serious responsibilities and duties of marriage and be physically, mentally and spiritually ready for this vocation. Often people who are not mature enough for this serious commitment endanger their happiness in time and in eternity by getting married too young. For this reason, the Church wisely discourages teen-age marriages.

The Sacrament of Matrimony makes the home a "little church." It gives special graces that help married people fulfill their duties to God, to each other and to their offspring. As husband and wife strive to become saints, they willingly accept and care for the children God sends them. Married couples who share the same faith and agree on religious and moral principles can more easily help one another form, educate and train their children.

Catholic homes, as miniature churches, should reflect the holiness, love, obedience and joy of the Holy Family. Through the Sacrament of Matrimony, parents and children are joined in Christ by faith and grace. Together, as a small family of God, they form an image of the universal Church in which the parents receive the authority of Jesus and each member strives to live His life.

Catholic families that are bound to God and each other in time can confidently look forward to being reunited for all eternity in heaven, their true home.

Matrimony is a sacrament by which
a baptized man and a baptized woman
bind themselves together in Christ
in a special way, for the rest of their lives.

REVIEW QUESTIONS

1. Who instituted marriage?

God instituted and blessed marriage from the beginning of time and gave it certain purposes and laws.

2. What is Matrimony?

Matrimony is the sacrament by which a baptized man and

a baptized woman bind themselves together in Christ in a special way for life. Through this sacrament, husband and wife live together in God's grace and imitate and represent Christ's own love for His Church.: As the sacrament of family life, Matrimony makes the home a "little church."

3. Who made marriage a sacrament?

Jesus Christ made marriage one of the seven sacraments of His Church. By doing so, He raised its dignity.

4. What does the Sacrament of Matrimony do for a husband and wife?

The Sacrament of Matrimony gives a husband and wife the graces they need to obey God's Commandments and the laws of the Church, particularly those concerning marriage.

Specifically, it enables them to do the following:

1. Glorify God in their mutual love for each other.
2. Extend God's family by accepting and caring for the children He gives them.
3. Educate their children in the true faith.

5. How long does marriage last?

Marriage lasts until the death of one of the partners. The Church forbids remarriage after divorce or separation as long as one of the partners of marriage is living. Because the

Sacrament of Matrimony binds a husband and wife to each other in Christ for life, the bonds of a true sacramental marriage can only be broken by death.

6. At what age should a person marry?

Ideally a person should marry when he is physically, mentally, spiritually, emotionally and socially ready to accept the serious responsibilities of the married vocation. Since all people do not mature at the same age, it is difficult to suggest a specific age when young people should marry. But the Church strongly discourages teen-age marriages because most teenagers are not ready for marriage. By marrying too soon, people risk their happiness in time and in eternity.

7. Should Catholics marry Catholics?

Yes, Catholics should marry Catholics. The American Bishops in *Basic Teachings for Catholic Religious Education* state: "It should be made clear that the Church discourages the contracting of mixed marriages in order to encourage a full union of mind and life in matrimony. "

8. Why did God institute marriage?

God instituted marriage so that a husband and wife would love each other in the way He intended and enlarge God's family by having children and educating them in the true faith.

9. Where should Catholics be married?

Catholics should be married in a Catholic Church in the presence of witnesses. Catholics who "attempt" marriage outside the Church WITHOUT an authorized Catholic priest as the chief witness and WITHOUT a dispensation from the bishop, are entering a sinful state and are not considered by the Church as lawfully married in the mind of God.

DISCUSSION QUESTIONS

1. How long does marriage last?
2. Why does the Church strongly discourage "teen-age marriages"?
3. What is a "mixed marriage"?
4. What is the Church's official teaching on "mixed marriages"? Explain.
5. What did Jesus teach about marriage, divorce and remarriage?
6. Does the Catholic Church forbid divorce and remarriage? Explain.
7. If a person gets a court divorce after he has been truly married, is he still married in the eyes of God? Explain.
8. What laws of God and the Church concerning marriage must Catholics understand before they enter into the marriage state?

●●●

FOR OLDER STUDENTS

Matrimony is one man and one woman entering into a sacred covenant with each other in a partnership ordered toward the good of each other and the procreation and education of children. Their covenant agreement is irrevocable. The indissolubility of a true sacramental marriage has always been taught by the Catholic Church in its tradition and the sacred scriptures.

Jesus Christ raised the marriage covenant for a baptized man and woman to the dignity of a sacrament. Performing the duties of marriage therefore assists the couple in growing in holiness and is a help to heaven. The sacrament gives them spiritual strength to carry the burdens of married life.

God is the author of marriage. There was written into the very nature of man and woman as they came from their Creator the vocation to marriage. Man and woman are created in the image and likeness of God, from the love of God and as such are given the vocation to love one another. With the coming of Jesus Christ, the Word made flesh to redeem us and the raising of marriage to a sacrament, St. Paul could say: "Husbands, love your wives, as Christ loved the Church. ... This is a great mystery, and I mean in reference to Christ and the Church" (Eph 5:25, 32).

The union of husband and wife sanctified with the sacrament of Matrimony signifies Christ's own union with His Church. The sacrament thus perfects human love, makes it sanctifying in Christ unto eternal life and strengthens their marriage bond so that it is indissoluble. Marriage is not a private thing but establishes the couple in a holy and public state of life in the Church. It is fitting that their marriage celebration be public within a liturgical celebration. It must be before a priest, or a witness authorized by the Church as well as other witnesses.

For a marriage to be valid, the couple entering marriage must be willing to give themselves to each other in a unity, an openness to fertility, and with the mature concept that their union is indissoluble until death. Sexuality in marriage becomes a sign and pledge of spiritual communion. Husband and wife thus give themselves to each other so that it concerns the innermost being of the human person.

If a couple entered marriage attaching conditions to their marriage, making it a trial marriage, or the intention to use means permanently to avoid children, when physically they were capable of having children, such a marriage would be invalid. The refusal of fertility turns married life away from the child which is the supreme gift of married love.

Artificial birth control is mortally sinful. Couples may practice natural family planning for serious reasons. Natural family planning is within the laws of God and His Church and is in harmony with nature, not opposed to it. Spouses to whom God does not grant children can still have a conjugal life and their marriage can radiate fruitfulness in charity, hospitality and sacrifice in various ways.

A married person who divorces from a living, lawful spouse and marries another outside the Church is going contrary to the plan and law of God as taught by Jesus Christ. While such persons are still members of the Church they cannot receive Holy Communion while living in an invalid marriage. Such unfortunate persons are encouraged to do what they can, attend Mass, participate in the Church as far as possible and educate their children in the fullness of faith.

There is no such thing allowed by God as a marriage

between persons of the same sex. It is contrary to the natural law. Sacred Scripture presents homosexual acts as acts of grave depravity. The tradition of the Church has always taught that homosexual acts are intrinsically disordered. Those with such tendencies should be accepted with respect. At the same time homosexual persons are called to chastity and by self-mastery with the help of prayer and sacramental grace they can gradually approach Christian perfection.

Ideally a Catholic should marry another Catholic who is committed to the Catholic faith so that the true faith is communicated effectively to children. The difficulties of mixed marriages must not be underestimated less the temptation of religious indifference arise and children are not educated and formed in the Catholic faith. Jesus Christ was born into a human family. The Holy Family is thus a model for Christian families. At the beginning of the Church Christian families who became believers were islands of Christian life in an unbelieving and hostile world. Modern times often reflect the same hostile environment. The Second Vatican Council used the ancient expression by calling the family the "Domestic Church." In the family parents by word and example are to be the first heralds of the faith to their children.

Catechism of the Catholic Church: 1601 - 1666; 2357 - 2359, 2382.

Bible: Gen 1:28, 31, 2:18-25; Cor 7:39; Eph 5:25-26; 31-32; Mt 5:31-32; 19:3 -11; 11:29-30 Mk 8:34; 10: 10:9; 11-12; Lk 16:18; Acts 11:14; 16:31; 1 Cor 7:10-11.

Questions to answer:

1. What is a true marriage in the eyes of the Church?
2. Why is "marriage" between persons of the same sex impossible?
3. What are the effects of the sacrament of Matrimony?
4. Name some conditions a couple may have before marriage which would make their attempted marriage invalid?
5. Could a true sacramental marriage ever be dissolved?
6. Is an annulment the same as a marriage being dissolved? Explain the meaning of annulment.
7. What is the difference between artificial birth control and natural family planning?
8. What could be the difficulties in a mixed marriage?
9. What is the supreme gift of married love?
10. How is the Christian family a domestic church?

●●●

POINTS FOR PARENTS AND TEACHERS

The sanctity, dignity and indissolubility of marriage and the evil of divorce should be inculcated into the Christian conscience at a very early age. Such teachings should be repeated and enlarged upon at various stages of life so that these basic concepts may become a part of one's thinking and living. (This approach is sometimes called the Concentric Method in education.)

Young Catholics should realize that, as Catholics. they must be different from other people in many ways. For instance, they cannot follow the dictates of an atheistic, non-Christian or materialis-

tic society if they are to be authentic Catholic Christians.

Even young children need to have a right understanding of family life and an appreciation of the sacredness of marriage. They should know that the Sacrament of Matrimony makes the home a "little church," and the family a miniature "mystical body." Young Catholics should be taught that marriage is for mature adults. All these values should be instilled during the early grade school years, before children become prejudiced in their thinking or wrongly influenced.

The ideal of Catholics marrying Catholics and the reason for this should also be explained. Steady dating that is exclusive should be discouraged for high school students. Realizing that dating is intended to be a preparation for marriage and not merely "for fun," young Catholics should try to date Catholics whenever this is possible. Wholesome values that are taught and practiced during childhood and adolescent years help mold and strengthen adults to live successful, productive lives.

Parents and educators should instruct young Catholics that the proper place for them to marry is in a Catholic Church before an authorized Catholic priest. Those teaching the Sacrament of Matrimony must not forget Church law or make the mistake of emphasizing what is only a DISPENSATION from Church law. Sometimes in stressing the need for a dispensation, which is both necessary and important in the case of mixed marriages, some forget to teach that the Church's first choice, as stated in Church law, is that Catholics should marry Catholics. But even when the proper dispensation has been granted for a mixed marriage, the Catholic party is still obliged to do all in his power to share his faith and must have ALL his children baptized and reared as Catholics.

There has been much misunderstanding about these matters in recent years. Those instructing Catholic youth about marriage must make it clear that a Catholic in a mixed marriage must promise to have ALL the children baptized and educated as Catholics. Also, the normal place, even for mixed marriages, is in a Catholic Church before a Catholic priest. Young people must be taught that dating is not simply a social or "fun" experience—it is a preparation for marriage. That is why Catholics should try to date Catholics.

LESSON 23
SACRAMENTALS

Sacramentals are holy objects or actions of the Church which obtain grace and temporal favors for men from God through the prayers of the Church.

Most Catholics are familiar with sacramentals such as: crucifixes; holy water; pictures or statues of Our Lord, the Blessed Virgin Mary, the saints or angels; blessed ashes and palms; medals; Rosaries and Scapulars. However, many do not realize that the blessing of a priest or bishop and exorcisms (the freeing from the powers of the devil or evil spirits) are also powerful sacramentals of the Church.

Sometimes sacramentals are called "little sacraments" because they are like the sacraments in some ways. However, they are also very different.

For example, the seven sacraments are signs in which the very Person of Jesus Christ is present, acts and gives grace. But the Person of Christ is NOT present in sacramentals. The sacraments have Jesus' POWER in themselves, but any spiritual power connected with sacramentals comes only from God through the prayers of the Church and never from the objects themselves.

Holy objects become sacramentals after a priest or bishop blesses them. When Catholics use or wear sacramentals with the RIGHT disposition, they can receive many benefits, such

*Sacramentals are holy objects or actions
of the Church which obtain grace and
temporal favors from God through
the prayers of the Church.*

as: actual graces, the remission of temporal punishment due to sin, the forgiveness of venial sins, protection from evil spirits and other blessings of body and soul.

By the priest's blessing, sacramentals are set aside for spiritual purposes and the prayers of the Church are offered for those who use them. Although Catholics should treat sacramentals with devotion and care, they must never think of them as good luck charms, for that would be superstitious and sinful. Instead, sacramentals should be used with faith, love and full knowledge that all blessings and grace come from God alone.

Since the modern world uses numerous signs and symbols, it should not be difficult for Catholics to understand, accept and value the many signs the Church uses to remind others of its identity with Christ. Indeed, sacramentals are signs which remind people to lift up their minds and hearts to God.

For instance, holy water should help Catholics remember their Baptism and the tremendous graces they received when they first became members of Christ's Mystical Body. This same sacramental is also a powerful weapon against evil.

The priest in blessing it asks God to protect the places where it is used and prays that the devil will have no power over those who use it. Catholics should not only bless themselves with holy water each time they enter and leave God's House, the Church; they should also use it frequently at home.

Indeed, Catholics can witness for Christ (and gain many blessings, too) by wearing and using sacramentals as outward signs of their interior love and devotion to God. Crucifixes, holy water, sacred pictures, statues, blessed candles, etc., should be a part of every Catholic home. These and other sacramentals remind people of God and often inspire them to know, love and serve Him better.

REVIEW QUESTIONS

1. What are sacramentals?

Sacramentals are holy objects or actions instituted by the Church which obtain grace and temporal favors for men from God through the prayers of the Church.

Sacramentals inspire devotion if they are used properly. They also stir up dispositions in the hearts of men which invite God's graces. Unlike the sacraments, sacramentals do not have power in themselves; rather, their effects come from God through the prayers of the Church.

2. What sacramentals are most frequently used by Catholics?

The following sacramentals are most frequently used by Catholics: Rosaries, Scapulars, holy water, candles, blessed ashes, blessed palms, crucifixes, medals and statues or pictures of Our Lord, the Blessed Virgin Mary and the saints.

The Stations of the Cross in Parish Churches and the church building itself are also sacramentals. The very appearance of a Catholic Church should remind Catholics to lift up their minds and hearts to God.

3. Should objects intended to be used as sacramentals be blessed?

Yes, objects intended to be used as sacramentals should be blessed. In fact, it is the priest's blessing that really makes them sacramentals and sets them aside for spiritual purposes.

Catholics should always feel free to ask priests to bless objects intended for religious purposes. Once they are blessed, such objects should be shown special reverence and never used in a superstitious way. The prayers of the Church become effective when sacramentals are used with faith and devotion.

4. Have the American Bishops encouraged Catholics to use sacramentals?

Yes, the American Bishops have encouraged Catholics to use sacramentals. On November 21, 1973, the Catholic Bishops of the United States issued a Pastoral Letter on the Blessed Virgin Mary, entitled "Behold Your Mother, Woman of Faith."

In it, the Bishops called for a place in the Catholic Church building "for a fitting image of the Mother of the Lord." Our Bishops reminded us that Pope Paul VI had also recently stated that the Rosary and the Brown Scapular were among the tested forms of devotion that bring Catholics closer to Christ through the example and protection of His Holy Mother. The Bishops also mentioned the "Miraculous Medal" given to St. Catherine Laboure in 1830 and spoke of the Apparition of Our Lady of Guadalupe in 1531. The miraculous picture of Our Lady given to us by heaven is a highly honored sacramental which now hangs in the new Basilica (Church) of Our Lady of Guadalupe in Mexico City.

Our American Bishops considered the appearances of Our Lady mentioned above and those at Fatima in 1917 as "authenticated" or true and worthy of belief. Therefore, Catholics should heed the requests of the Mother of God at Fatima by praying the Rosary daily and wearing the Brown Scapular of Our Lady of Mt. Carmel as a sign of their devotion to her Immaculate Heart.

DISCUSSION QUESTIONS

1. Name some sacramental "actions" of the Church. Explain each.

2. Name some commonly used sacramentals that are "holy objects."

3. How are sacraments and sacramentals alike?

4. How do sacraments and sacramentals differ?

5. What would you say to a young Catholic who was proud to wear a secular peace symbol but ashamed to carry the Rosary or wear a blessed medal or the Brown Scapular?

6. What benefits can be received from using or wearing sacramentals?

7. What is the "right" or "proper" way to use sacramentals?

8. Under what circumstances would sacramentals be misused or abused?

9. Why is holy water such a powerful sacramental?

10. Name some special times when holy water should be used.

●●●

FOR OLDER STUDENTS

Sacramentals bear a resemblance to the sacraments. The sacramentals do not give the grace of the Holy Spirit in the same way the sacraments do. Their spiritual effects are obtained through the prayers of the Church. Each of the seven sacraments was instituted by Jesus Christ Himself. The sacramentals are also sacred signs but were instituted by the Church. Their proper use dispose men to receive the effects of the sacraments. Blessings can be used to sanctify different circumstances of life.

Blessing with holy water recalls Baptism. We entered the Church through Baptism and the custom of blessing ourselves with holy water as we enter the church building recalls this.

Among sacramentals blessings rank first; blessings of persons, meals, objects, and places. The Church imparts blessings by invoking the name of Jesus Christ and usually making the sign of the cross.

Certain blessings consecrate persons to God, or the blessings set objects and places aside for liturgical worship. There are special blessings for the abbot or abbess of a monastery; the consecration of virgins, the rite of profession for the religious life. Certain ministries of the Church may receive a special blessing: readers, acolytes, catechists, etc. There is a special blessing of a church or an altar and of things used for the sacraments; examples: holy oils, chalices, Mass vestments, bells.

The Church has the rite of exorcism whereby in the name of Jesus Christ it prays that a person or object be protected against the power of the Evil One and withdrawn from the devil's dominion. A simple form of exorcism is performed at the regular celebration of Baptism. Solemn exorcism, or "major exorcism" is performed only by a priest who has the permission of the bishop and rules of the Church in this must be followed. Solemn exorcism is directed to the expulsion of demons or freeing a person from diabolic possession; the authority of Jesus Christ which He entrusted to His Church is invoked in such cases.Popular sacramentals which are used to express the piety of the people must never replace the liturgical life of the Church which involves the sacraments which come from Jesus Christ Himself. Various forms of popular piety may be rooted in different peoples of different cultures. The Church is careful to foster only those which express an evangelical instinct and a human wisdom that can be elevated to be in harmony with the Christian life. The religious sense of the people has always found expression in piety and practices surrounding and resembling the Church's sacramental life; these include pilgrimages to shrines, religious processions, crucifixes, stations of the cross, statues, the rosary, psalms, scapulars, medals, etc.

Pope John Paul II stated that in modern times religious pilgrimages to shrines can do for Christian people what Monasteries did for Christians during the first millennium. Authentic shrines are eucharistic centered as their ultimate goal.

The veneration of authentic relics is approved by the Church. These may be objects connected with a saint, e.g., part of the body (small piece of bone) or clothing. Relics may not be bought or sold. These may be used in invoking the saint associated with them. There are also relics of the true cross. One must be careful that relics are authentic.

Catechism of the Catholic Church: 1667 - 1679.
Bible: Eph 1:3; Mk 125-26; 3:15; 6:7, 18; 16:17.

Questions to answer:

1. How do sacramentals bear resemblance to the sacraments?
2. How do sacramentals differ from the sacraments?
3. Explain the imbalance in the spirituality of a person who considered himself Catholic while giving great emphasis to sacramentals but who neglected regular participation in the divine liturgy of the Church.
4. What is meant by a major exorcism?

●●●

POINTS FOR PARENTS AND TEACHERS

Because modern man is so attuned to symbols and proudly wears objects that express his affiliation and approval, he should be able to understand why Catholics wear and use sacramentals.

Proper instruction on "sacramentals" can help young Catholics know their identity as children of God and members of His Church. However, parents and teachers must maintain a balanced approach in teaching this unit. Indeed, young people should be encouraged to carry the Rosary and wear blessed medals, Scapulars, crucifixes, etc. Such practices often reelect and instill a sense of devotion, faith and love in the hearts of those who use sacramentals and sometimes remind others of God. At the same time, adults must not lead young Catholics to think they have to use EVERY sacramental. This would be another extreme which should be avoided.

Because religious articles often bring grace and consolation to others, parents and teachers should give these as gifts and encourage their children and students to do the same. Such items can usually be obtained with little effort and expense from Catholic Religious Gift Stores or Parish Churches.

●●●

*Centuries after the Blessed Virgin Mary
gave the Brown Scapular to St. Simon Stock,
she presented it to the world again*

LESSON 24
THE CORPORAL
WORKS OF MERCY

When Jesus lived on earth 2,000 years ago, He always showed kindness, love, compassion and mercy to all men. Today His followers, Christians, must be "other Christs" and continue to reflect His love, goodness, concern and mercy to the world. This duty is mentioned in many parts of the Bible (I John 3:18, I Thessalonians 5:14-16, Tobias 4:7-12, Romans 12:9-21, etc.).

Jesus Himself said, "Not everyone who says to me, 'Lord, Lord,' shall enter the kingdom of heaven; but he who does the will of my Father..." (Matthew 7:21). God wills that men obey His Commandments and prove their love for Him.

Our Lord taught that it was necessary to earn heaven through His merits by doing good. Therefore, Christians who refuse to do good exclude themselves from the kingdom of God. In the Bible, St. James speaks about the need to perform acts of goodness when he says, "...faith...without works is dead" (James 2:26).

But good works "in themselves" do not justify or save men. They must be done in FAITH for a spiritual motive (such as fear of the Lord, hope, love or sorrow in Christ) in order to bring salvation.

Jesus said that anything done to another is really done to Him (Matthew 25:40). True Christians believe this. They see

Jesus living in the members of His Mystical Body, the Church, and respond to Him with love. At the same time, they permit Our Lord to act through them in time.

Any moral act of kindness or generosity done for a spiritual motive toward another is a GOOD WORK. Each, even the least, will be rewarded by God. Fasting, prayer, almsgiving and obedience to the laws of God and His Church are examples of good works. In addition, Christians are obliged to practice the CORPORAL and SPIRITUAL WORKS OF MERCY.

The CORPORAL WORKS OF MERCY are acts of love, coming from the heart, that help others in their PHYSICAL or BODILY needs. Men show their love of neighbor and belief that he is made in God's image and likeness by such deeds. There are seven chief Corporal Works of Mercy:

1. To feed the hungry.
2. To give drink to the thirsty.
3. To clothe the naked.
4. To visit the imprisoned.
5. To shelter the homeless.
6. To visit the sick.
7. To bury the dead.

Catholic Christians should give food, drink, clothing, shelter, medicine, etc., to those in need.

They must also work to correct wrongs or abuses that prevent men from having the necessities of life. Many people cannot earn a living because they do not have jobs. Others are not paid enough to support themselves or their families. Sometimes, persons are mistreated or denied their basic human rights because they have a different color skin or way of life.

Christians, like Christ, must love all men and have His

special concern for the poor. The Catholic Church, throughout its long history, has always tried to help those in spiritual and temporal need. Today it is making special efforts to teach the poor how to provide for their future needs so they can be self-sufficient.

Yes, if any person is hungry, thirsty, homeless, lonely, discouraged, sick or needy, he must be helped NOW in a practical way. Christians have the duty to be "other Christs" by performing the works of mercy and caring for their neighbor. In addition, they must work together to correct abuses so all people can earn a decent living throughout their entire lives and not merely be helped for a day, a week, a month or even a year.

What a great eternal reward awaits those who make sacrifices for others. In judging them, Our Lord will say: "...'Come, blessed of my Father, take possession of the kingdom prepared for you from the foundation of the world; for I was hungry and you gave me to eat...thirsty and you gave me to drink...a stranger and you took me in; naked and you covered me; sick and you visited me...in prison and you came to me.' Then the just will answer him, saying, 'Lord, when did we see thee hungry, and feed thee; or thirsty, and give thee drink? And when did we see thee a stranger, and take thee in; or naked and clothe thee...sick, or in prison, and come to thee?' And answering the king will say to them, 'Amen I say to you, as long as you did it for one of these, the least of my brethren, you did it for me'" (Matthew 25:34-40).

"As long as you did it for one of these,
the least of my brethren, you did it for me."
—Matthew 25:40

REVIEW QUESTIONS

1. What is meant by the "Corporal Works of Mercy"?

The Corporal Works of Mercy are acts of love that come from the heart and help others in their bodily needs. Catholics must recognize that all men are made in the image and likeness of God. Jesus has said that anything done for others in faith and love is done for Him. This is the way Christians should consider acts of love done for others.

2. Can men save their souls without doing good works?

No, men cannot save their souls without doing good works. However, good works in themselves do not cause men to be justified or saved. Rather, it is when good works are done out of faith or from a spiritual motive, such as: fear of the Lord, hope, love or sorrow in Christ, that men's works are saving.

Although Jesus Himself must first draw men to His heavenly Father in the unity of the Holy Spirit, they are always free to respond to His call or reject it. Catholics must have a living faith manifested in good works. The Apostle James puts it this way: "...faith...without works is dead" (James 2:26).

3. What are "good works"?

Good works are moral actions of kindness and generosity towards others which are done for a spiritual motive. They include: obeying the Commandments of God and the Church, prayer, fasting, almsgiving and the Corporal and Spiritual Works of Mercy. Each good work will be rewarded by God.

DISCUSSION QUESTIONS

1. Give at least one example of how each of the seven Corporal Works of Mercy can be practiced today.

2. Do good works in themselves cause men to be saved or justified? Explain.

3. Give some examples of "good works."

4. How are good works signs of faith?

5. Could a person do good works for a selfish, rather than a purely spiritual, reason? Explain.

6. Are Corporal Works of Mercy done for others really done for Jesus? Explain.

FOR OLDER STUDENTS

The Church has a doctrine of social justice which respects the dignity of each human person. Society should be ordered to the good of all human persons. We consider in this lesson briefly the Church's social doctrine in relationship to the corporal and finally, in the next lesson, the spiritual works of mercy. These works concern the good of the human person. The social doctrine of the Church developed especially during the nineteenth century when many problems arose in society and between nations because of the modern industrial revolution, new production of consumer goods, new concept of state and authority, new forms of labor and ownership and the development of a less and less rural society. The Church in developing her social doctrine also remained true to the permanent values of all her teachings and Tradition.

When social relationships are determined entirely by economic factors it is contrary to the nature of the human person and his acts. It is morally unacceptable to make profit the exclusive norm for economic activity. Disordered desire for money causes conflicts which disturb the social order. When the persons are looked upon only for means of profit it enslaves man, and contributes to the spread of atheism and the break down of family life.

The Church rejects totalitarian and atheistic ideologies of modern times which have lead to "communism" or "socialism." Individualism and the absolute primacy of the law of the marketplace over human labor often found under "capitalism" is rejected by the Church. There must be a reasonable regulation of the marketplace and economic initiatives, that respect the hierarchy of values which keep in mind the common good. The working man is entitled to a living wage for himself and to support his family. To exploit cheap labor for the sake of profit is contrary to human dignity, the rights of each individual and the decency of family living. Human persons don't exist for the good of an economic company or the State. Employers must consider the good of their employees. The

State exists to serve the common good of human persons.

Respect for the human person requires respect for the rights each one has from the Creator. All human authority which comes from God must be subject to authentic moral principles and for the good of others. Each one should be a neighbor to others and serve them where possible. In the case of the disadvantaged, the duty is even more urgent. "As you did it to one of the least of these my brethren, you did it to me." (Mt 25:40)

Christians must respect the dignity of all human persons regardless of their nationality, creed or culture. This duty extends to others who think or act differently than we do. Love must be extended even to enemies. We must love our enemies even though we hate the evil he may do.

There is equality among all human persons even though there are differences. All are created in the image of the one God, all have rational souls, the same origin and are called to the same destiny of heaven. All have been redeemed by Jesus Christ.

Human persons on coming into the world need the help of others to develop bodily skills and the spiritual life. Talents are not distributed equally and in God's plan those gifted with special talents and opportunities are to share the benefits with others in need. Often persons are obliged to be generous, kind, share goods and foster the mutual enrichment of cultures.

The principle of solidarity, sometimes referred to as "friendship" or "social charity," is required by Christian brotherhood. Solidarity is seen in the fair distribution of goods and proper remuneration for work. It is seen in a just social order where tensions are reduced by negotiation. There should be solidarity between the rich and the poor, workers among themselves; between employers and employees. Nations must work together in solidarity for the good of all their citizens.

Catechism of the Catholic Church: 1928 - 1942; 2420; 2425.
Bible: Mt 5:43-44; 6:33; 25:14-30, 40; Lk 19:11-27.

Questions to answer:

1. What moved the Church to use her ancient faith and moral principles to develop a social doctrine in modern times?

2. What are dangers to the respect of the human person in unchecked "capitalism"?

3. What is the evil of a company or employer who hires cheap labor to make a great profit with no advantages going to the working persons?

4. Explain the Church's teachings on solidarity.

5. How does the social doctrine of the Church complement the corporal works of mercy?

POINTS FOR PARENTS AND TEACHERS

Much has been said and written about modern catechetics. Often religion is reduced to mere sociology when, for instance, students are taught to be kind to their neighbor but hear little about God or the supernatural motive for natural goodness.

Although the Church has always been concerned about social issues, Vatican II has particularly made Catholics aware of their responsibility in this regard. This lesson and the one to follow aim to present the balanced thinking and teaching of the Church on the need to perform BOTH the Corporal and Spiritual Works of Mercy.

For many centuries, great religious orders have been conspicuous for their efforts to practice the works of mercy. Catholic lay people, too, have been urged to do the same. No one ever considered these works as mere sociology or psychology because the Church for centuries has taught them in the context of the total faith, and Catholics have practiced them for a spiritual motive in Christ.

It is important that young Catholics be taught to perform the Corporal Works of Mercy. However, it is a serious mistake to stress the need for generosity, kindness and charity to others and fail to emphasize that such acts should be done to Christ in our neighbor from a spiritual motive. Once more, it is simply a matter of presenting our faith as "supernatural" and not merely "natural."

●●●

LESSON 25
THE SPIRITUAL WORKS OF MERCY

Those who truly love God do His will. They obey the Ten Commandments and the laws of the Church and show their love of neighbor by performing the Spiritual and Corporal Works of Mercy.

When God created man, He made him in His own image and likeness and gave him a body and soul. Christians who claim they love God, Whom they cannot see, prove this love when they do good to their neighbor, whom they can see. This means helping others in their physical or bodily needs as well as in their spiritual or "soul-touching" needs.

The Spiritual Works of Mercy mark Christians as true apostles of Jesus Christ. Such acts strengthen the Mystical Body and help save and sanctify souls. The seven chief "supernatural" or Spiritual Works of Mercy are:

1. To admonish the sinner.
2. To instruct the ignorant.
3. To counsel the doubtful.
4. To comfort the sorrowful.
5. To bear wrongs patiently.
6. To forgive all injuries.
7. To pray for the living and the dead.

*Each time a Christian prays
the "Our Father," he asks God
to forgive him his sins and says
that he, like Jesus, forgives all
who have offended him.*

To Admonish the Sinner

If others do wrong, Catholics are obliged to make them realize their error. Such corrections, however, must always be done with kindness and in the spirit of true charity or love.

Catholics "admonish sinners" when they tell them to correct bad habits, try to keep others from committing sin, encourage people to do good and give a good example.

To Instruct the Ignorant

Although parents, priests, sisters, missionaries and teachers in Catholic Schools and CCD classes have the special responsibility of instructing others about God, all lay people, and children, too, must be missionaries. Each person, regardless of his age or vocation, has special opportunities to talk to others about God and make Him better known, loved and served.

When a person really loves someone, he wants others to know him. Now, Catholic Christians who truly love God and His Church also desire to tell the world about Them. Why? Because they realize their teaching will glorify God, help save souls and make Jesus Christ better known and loved.

To Counsel the Doubtful

Many people need advice in order to know and do what is right. Persons in authority, especially bishops, priests, parents and teachers, have the duty to help those who are in doubt.

Often young Catholics, lacking the wisdom, training and

experience of older people, cannot counsel those in need. However, they can and should help in other ways. For instance, when young people realize their friends are having difficulties, they should encourage them to get help from persons who can assist them. But this is not all. They must also share the truths of their holy faith by good example, prayer and instruction.

To Comfort the Sorrowful

When people suffer any great natural or supernatural sorrow, such as: death in the family; pain that results from friends or relatives who refuse to obey God and practice their faith; sickness; loss of a job, friend or home, etc., they need to be comforted. In such cases, Catholic Christians must see Jesus sorrowing and do all they can to comfort and help their neighbor for love of God.

Each member of the Mystical Body has a vital part to play in consoling others and showing genuine Christian love and concern. As parents and adults comfort youth in their needs, so young people, too, must learn to be sympathetic and understanding to their friends and elders and try to avoid causing them sorrow.

To Bear Wrongs Patiently

No one bore more unjust accusations than Jesus, and no one was as innocent and guiltless as He. Yet, in all His sufferings Jesus remained meek, humble and gentle. He even took the sins of all men upon Himself without any complaint, in love.

Christians must be true followers of Christ and imitate Him in all things. By doing so, they will earn many graces for themselves and merit in Jesus' Name the conversion of sinners. Whenever Catholic Christians are falsely accused or treated unkindly, they should always remember to accept their wrongs patiently and offer them to God with love.

To Forgive All Injuries

When Jesus was dying on the Cross, He prayed for His executioners saying, "...'Father, forgive them, for they do not know what they are doing'..." (Luke 23:34). Each time Christians pray the "Our Father," they ask God to forgive them their sins (trespasses) and state that they, likewise, forgive all who have wronged or offended them.

God is merciful to those who are merciful to their neighbor. Therefore, Catholics must forgive all, even those who have injured them deliberately.

This means they should never carry a grudge or refuse to make up or repair injuries.

To Pray for the Living and the Dead

Our heavenly Father is pleased when the members of His Mystical Body, the Church, pray for each other. Indeed, it is through the Communion of Saints that the souls in heaven, on earth and in purgatory help one another by means of prayer.

Young Catholics must remember their duty to ask God's

blessings and graces for the Pope, their bishop, parish priests, parents, brothers, sisters, teachers and friends. They should also pray for the dying, the suffering souls in purgatory and poor sinners. Praying for others is a most POWERFUL gift and act of love.

REVIEW QUESTIONS

1. In addition to saving their own soul, what other spiritual obligation do Christians have?

In addition to saving their own soul, Christians have the serious obligation to do all they can to be instruments of Jesus in the salvation of other souls. This means they must **practice the Spiritual** Works of Mercy whenever and wherever they can.

2. What is meant by the "Spiritual Works of Mercy"?

The Spiritual Works of Mercy are good works done for others that directly help the spirit or soul. They affect the eternal welfare of others and are directed to help others glorify God and save their soul through the infinite merits of Jesus Christ.

3. Could a person save his own soul if he refused to perform the Spiritual Works of Mercy?

No, a person could not save his own soul if he refused to perform the Spiritual Works of Mercy. Everyone has the obligation to do good for others whenever and wherever this is possible.

Christians must be concerned about the entire person of others. They must work with faith and love to show their regard for their neighbor. Every human person is composed of body and soul. Therefore, both the Corporal and Spiritual Works of Mercy must be performed in love and faith to witness for Christ in the members of His Mystical Body.

DISCUSSION QUESTIONS

1. Name the seven Spiritual Works of Mercy. Explain each.

2. Give at least one practical example of how young Catholics today could perform each of the seven Spiritual Works of Mercy.

3. How are the Spiritual Works of Mercy like the Corporal Works of Mercy?

4. How do the Spiritual Works of Mercy differ from the Corporal Works of Mercy?

●●●

FOR OLDER STUDENTS

The virtue of solidarity does not concern our neighbor only in regard to material goods. The Church promotes concern about their spiritual goods as well. This has often had the effect of opening doors for the development of temporal goods. Charity brings people to work together for the good of one and all. Jesus said: "Seek first his kingdom and his righteousness, and all these things shall be yours as well" (Mt 6:33).

During two thousands years of Christianity the Church has prompted souls to heroic charity as monasteries in Europe often did with surrounding farmers. Before the advancement of modern technology the monks, who were educated in various fields of knowledge also grew in agricultural knowledge, through sharing in charity and experimentation and then instructed farmers of the area in agricultural practices.

The Church in preaching the gospel has fostered help of the sick, helped the poor, helped the development of civilization, and science for the good of all peoples so as to make life worthy of the dignity of man and the Christian.

The Spiritual Works of Mercy stem from the Church's realization that all have been called to beatitude although wounded by sin. The Church teaches the rules of conduct which lead to the promised beatitude. Christians live under the New Law of Jesus Christ whereby the grace of the Holy Spirit is received by faith in Jesus Christ operating in charity. The perfect life in Christ that reaches out to others in mercy is expressed above all in the Lord's Sermon on the Mount. The whole Law of the Gospel in found in Jesus' "new commandment" to love one another as He has loved us.

Catechism of the Catholic Church :1942; 1967 -1974.
Bible: Jn 15:12, 15; 13:34; Rom 8:15; 12:9-13; Gal 4:1-7.

Questions to answer:

1. How can concern for others' spiritual welfare sometimes contribute as well to temporal welfare?

2. During the first millennium especially, how were monasteries helpful to a rural society regarding the Corporal and Spiritual Works of Mercy?

3. Which teaching of Jesus Christ especially fosters the living of the perfect Christian life leading to eternal happiness?

4. Name one commandment given us by Jesus Christ whereby, if practiced, will fulfill the whole of the Law of the Gospel.

●●●

POINTS FOR PARENTS AND TEACHERS

"Love" is a popular word today. Unfortunately, it is not always properly understood. It is too often reduced to a natural experience only, and sometimes even to mere sense pleasure. Parents, as primary educators of children, and teachers, as their helpers, should instruct and form Catholic youth in the authentic Catholic meaning and practice of Christian charity which can be found in the practice of the Corporal and Spiritual Works of Mercy.

How strong Catholic education and formation would be

if parents would discuss such topics as the Spiritual Works of Mercy with their children! Sad to say, many think this responsibility lies with someone else.

Parents who read and are informed about the problems of modern religious education know that much criticism has been leveled at Catholic Schools and various Religious Educational Programs for their failures to teach and form youth in the faith. But at the same time, parents must point the finger of accusation at themselves if they do not do their part in educating their children in the faith at home.

Ideally there should be a union of altar, home and school. All three should stress the fullness of the true faith. However, the one that is FIRST and most IMPORTANT is the HOME. Although the teaching of parents may be less formal, it can be more effective and lasting. Good example and real family discussion on the faith and its practice are vital in the religious education and formation of Catholic youth.

Christians must see Jesus
sorrowing in their neighbors
and seek to comfort them.

Jesus Christ established only ONE Church, the Catholic Church, nearly 2,000 years ago. He did this by making St. Peter the first Pope and giving His twelve Apostles the authority to rule and teach in His Name. The authority of Jesus still remains in the world today. It has been handed down through the centuries to other Catholic Popes and bishops. In all, there have been 262 Popes in the Catholic Church. Their names and the years they reigned as Vicar of Christ have been recorded in history.

All reliable historians agree that the Catholic Church is the first (and therefore the oldest) of all Christian churches. In fact, the very first history of the Church is recorded in the Bible. In the "Acts of the Apostles," St. Luke describes the growth and development of the Church Christ founded. St. Matthew clearly states that Jesus promised He would be with His Church until the end of time and that He told His Apostles to take His Church to all nations.

After Our Lord established His Church on earth, He ascended into heaven. Since then, the history of man's salvation has been woven into the over-all history of the world.

The word "catholic" means universal or "all nations." Jesus commanded that the true faith be taught to all nations (Matthew 28:19-20). St. Ignatius of Antioch, who lived at the end of the first century, was already calling Christ's Church the "Catholic Church" because even then it was spreading to all parts of the known world.

Our Lord not only said His Church was to be an "All Nations Church," He also called this supernatural organization HIS Church and made St. Peter its visible head on earth (Matthew 16:18). Jesus promised that His Church would never be destroyed, not even by the powers of hell. Furthermore, He said He would send the Holy Spirit to keep the Church always in truth.

The only Church that could possibly be the Church Jesus founded is the one that has been in the world for almost 2,000 years. The Catholic Church is that old and still has a successor to St. Peter, its first Pope. If the Catholic Church were only of man and not willed and protected by God, it certainly would have been destroyed long ago.

Jesus Christ did not start many churches. He established only ONE Church. All educated historians agree that the Catholic Church IS the ancient Church. Although it is possible for some people in Jesus' Church to lose their faith (either entirely or in part), it is IMPOSSIBLE for the entire Church of Christ to be destroyed.

Indeed, there have been some very difficult and trying periods in the history of God's Church. Unfortunately, all Catholics have not remained faithful and obedient. Many disagreed with the true teachings of the Church and went so far as to break away from it. In the eleventh century, some eastern Catholics broke away and formed what is now called the "Orthodox churches." Various groups of Christians, called Protestants, left the ancient Catholic Church in the sixteenth century. Throughout the ages, there have been even further

"But you shall receive the power of the Holy Spirit coming upon you, and you shall be witnesses unto me in Jerusalem, and in all Judea and Samaria, and even to the uttermost part of the earth."

Acts 1:8

St. Luke describes the growth and development of the Church in the "Acts of the Apostles."

divisions among those who separated from the true Church.

Although the Catholic Church is the only Church that contains the FULL deposit of faith, all Christian churches (even though they have separated themselves from the true Church Jesus founded) possess SOME of God's truth. Catholics believe the Protestant churches lost more of Jesus' power and truth than the Orthodox churches because Protestants lost some of the sacraments (in addition to other important teachings), whereas the Orthodox mainly lost their belief in the Pope as the visible head of the Church on earth.

During difficult periods when it seemed as if the Church would certainly be destroyed, Jesus kept His promise and preserved it. Furthermore, He always will—for God, Who cannot deceive or be deceived has said, "...thou art Peter, and upon

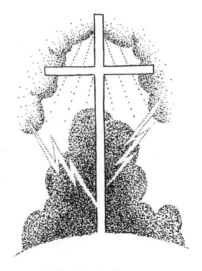

*"The blood of martyrs
is the seed of Christianity."*

this rock I will build my Church, and the gates of hell shall not prevail against it" (Matthew 16:18). Therefore, the Catholic Church with the fullness of the true faith will remain until the end of the world.

●●●

REVIEW QUESTIONS

1. Who founded the Catholic Church?

Jesus Christ, Our Lord and Savior, founded the Catholic Church when He lived on earth almost 2,000 years ago. Jesus established the Catholic Church upon the Apostles and made St. Peter the head and first Pope of His Church.

2. Can the Catholic Church ever be entirely destroyed?

No, the Catholic Church CANNOT ever be entirely destroyed because Jesus promised He would be with His Church all days, even until the end of the world. Our Lord also promised that the Holy Spirit would keep the Catholic Church in the truth under the leadership of the Pope.

The Catholic Church has suffered many trials since it was founded. In almost every century, men have risen up to say that the Church would be destroyed and disappear from the face of the earth before another century began. But the Church still survives and continues to grow.

Although some members, even large areas or whole countries, may fall away from the true faith, the universal Catholic Church established by Christ will never be destroyed.

Today many enemies and evil forces, both within and outside the Church, would like to change the Church so it would no longer be the true Church of Jesus Christ. However, if Catholics are obedient and follow the teachings of the Pope, they will be faithful to truth.

3. How many different kinds of Christian churches are there in the world today?

There are over 450 different kinds of Christian churches in the world today.

4. How did the many different kinds of Christian churches begin?

The many different kinds of Christian churches in the world today came into being when Christians disagreed and failed to live in harmony, peace and obedience. Protestantism, which began in the sixteenth century and includes hundreds of different denominations, was not the very first break from the Catholic Church.

As early as 320 A.D., a priest, Arius of Alexandria, denied the divinity of the Son of God and taught that Jesus Christ was ONLY a man. This false teaching or heresy was known as Arianism.

The Macedonian heresy stated that the Holy Spirit was not God. About 400 A.D., Pelagianism denied original sin and the necessity of grace. The Nestorian heresy taught that Christ had two persons, human and divine, rather than two natures in ONE divine Person. It also denied that Mary was the real Mother of God. The Monophysites wrongly said that Christ had only a divine nature and not a human nature. If the Monophysites were right, Christ Jesus could not have died on the Cross because God could not die as God but only as man in Jesus. The Iconoclasts, who were sometimes called image breakers, attacked the use and veneration of holy images.

In the ninth century, the Greek Schism broke out among the Christians. Their followers, now called Orthodox, kept a true priesthood but denied the authority of the Pope as the supreme and visible head of the universal Church on earth.

It would take many books to record, in detail, all the breaks from the one true Church. To summarize, history clearly shows what happened when people were not united in one faith under the one visible head of the Church on earth, the Pope.

The Roman Catholic Church is the only Church in the world that was established by the God-Man, Jesus Christ. All other churches were founded by men in time. All reliable historians agree that the Catholic Church is the first and oldest Christian Church. It has existed since the days of Jesus and His Apostles and is almost 2,000 years old. Catholics believe that ONLY the Catholic Church has the fullness of the one true faith.

DISCUSSION QUESTIONS

1. Who started the Roman Catholic Church?
2. Can it be proved that the Catholic Church is the oldest and first Church? Explain.
3. What does the word "catholic" mean?
4. How did the hundreds of other Christian churches begin?
5. Can individual Catholics lose their faith? Explain.
6. What must Catholics do to protect and preserve their Catholic Faith?
7. Do Catholics believe that the Orthodox churches lost more of Jesus' power and truth than the Protestant churches? Explain.
8. Do the Christian churches that have separated from the true Church Jesus founded possess ALL of God's truth? Explain.

●●●

FOR OLDER STUDENTS

Any authentic study of Church history involves a consideration of the apostolicity of the Church. The treasure of the Good News given the apostles by Jesus Christ has been protected by their successors for 2000 years. With the commission to take the Gospel to all nations the apostles left bishops as their successors. Early Fathers of the Church, such as St. Irenaeus, wrote that the bishops were given "their own position of teaching authority." (Adv. haeres, 3,3, 1). Furthermore, the early Fathers explicitly taught that "the apostolic preaching, which is expressed in a special way in the inspired books, was to be preserved in a continuous line of succession until the end of time."

There must be apostolic succession, through the sacrament of Holy Orders, to maintain the bond of unity in the family of God in the fullness of true faith with the divine powers Jesus gave His Church. Only the Roman Catholic Church has such an uninterrupted history in continuous succession. It truly became "Catholic" on the day of Pentecost and will always remain so until the second coming of Jesus Christ at the end of the world.

When the Church had been established less than a hundred years, St. Ignatius of Antioch (d. c. 107), bishop of Antioch in Syria for 40 years, could write: "Where there is Christ Jesus, there is the Catholic Church," (*Ad Smyrn.* 8,2: *Apostolic Fathers*, II/2,311).

The Church is said to be "Roman Catholic", since the Pope lives at Vatican City, within Rome, and true apostolicity in every sense requires union with the successor of St. Peter, the first pope so appointed by Jesus Christ Himself during His earthly life. A Roman Catholic recognizes the authority given St. Peter and present now in the Pope at Rome.

The Roman Catholic Church remains apostolic in three ways:

1. She was built on the foundation of the Apostles.
2. She keeps the deposit of faith intact with the help of the Holy Spirit dwelling in her as Soul of the Church.
3. She continues to be taught, sanctified and guided by the apostles through their successors which the apostles set up as the college of bishops, assisted by priests, who are in union with the successor of Peter, the supreme pastor.

St. Augustine wrote: "[The Church] has received the keys of the Kingdom of heaven so that, in her, sins may be forgiven through Christ's blood and the Holy Spirit's action..." (Sermo 214, 11).

The Catechism of the Catholic Church states: "The Church is in history, but at the same time she transcends it. It is only with the eyes of faith that one can see her in her visible reality and at the same time in her spiritual reality as bearer of divine life." (770)

Catechism of the Catholic Church: 3, 77, 770, 815, 830, 857, 971.

Bible: Eph 1:22-23; 4:3; 2:20; Acts 1:18; 2:42: Mt 28: 16-20; 1 Cor 9:1; 15:7-8; 2 Cor 5:18; Gal 1:1; etc.; 2 Tim 1:13-14.

Questions to answer:

1. Why is the Church called "apostolic"?

2. Explain how the study of the 2000 year history of the Church is complimentary to the apostolicity of the Church.

3. Why is apostolic succession essential to the fullness of true faith and all that Jesus gave His Church?

4. If the true Church is for all nations why is it called "Roman" Catholic?

●●●

POINTS FOR PARENTS AND TEACHERS

Parents and teachers should not make young people prejudiced against other Christians. Lesson 27 will help build proper attitudes in this regard. At the same time, young Catholics should study Church history in order to understand their Catholic identity and heritage. This study should continue throughout adolescence and adulthood.

LESSON 27
ECUMENISM: OTHER CHRISTIANS

In the very first centuries A.D., all Christians belonged to the Catholic Church which Jesus established. However, in the eleventh and sixteenth centuries, BIG breaks from the true Church took place which still exist today. First the Orthodox (eleventh century), then the Protestants (sixteenth century) separated from the Church.

Orthodox Christians, sometimes called Eastern Orthodox because they are mainly found in the eastern part of the world, are very much like Catholics. Even though they broke their union with the Pope at Rome, they still kept bishops who were truly ordained and consecrated. Therefore, Orthodox bishops and priests today have valid orders and possess the same powers that Jesus gave the first Apostles. They are truly part of the APOSTOLIC CHAIN.

The Orthodox Church also has ALL the true sacraments and their Mass is really the Sacrifice of the Cross perpetuated. Thus, when Orthodox Christians receive Holy Communion, they, too, receive the LIVING Body, Blood, Soul and Divinity of Jesus Christ, just as Catholics do.

After the Orthodox separated from the Catholic Church, some of their churches, called EASTERN RITE CATHOLICS, returned to the fullness of Jesus' Church by once more recognizing the Pope at Rome as the chief Bishop of the world and the visible head of the Church on earth.

*In the eleventh and sixteenth centuries, big breaks
from the true Church took place which still exist today.
First the Orthodox, then the Protestants separated
from the Catholic Church.*

Eastern Rite Catholics are ONE in faith with Catholics in every respect. Catholics should pray that all Orthodox churches, too, will soon become completely one with them in Christ. Some Eastern rite Catholics, such as the Maronite Catholics, have never been separated from the Pope.

Through the Sacrament of Baptism, Protestants are also united in Christ to Catholics and Orthodox Christians. Catholics believe that in most cases Protestant Christians are truly baptized into the Lord, Jesus Christ. This is possible because it is NOT necessary to have the powers of HOLY ORDERS to baptize. Although Protestants and Catholics share many of the same beliefs, they disagree on some very basic and important matters of faith. Often the differences that separate them arise from their understanding of God's revealed truths.

But Catholics and Protestants both look forward to Jesus' coming in glory at the end of the world. However, the Catholic Church teaches that Protestants do not have the Sacrament of Holy Orders, although they can in some way give faith to union with Jesus when they have a worship service in memory of the Lord's Supper.

God loves all people and wants them to be united with Him in one family and one Church. Catholics, Orthodox and Protestants are truly brothers and sisters in Christ, but only the Catholic Church possesses the fullness of the true faith.

Today there is a movement for unity among Christians called ECUMENISM. Its purpose is to work for greater understanding between Catholics and Protestants, Catholics and Orthodox, Orthodox and Protestants and between Protestants themselves, for there are over 400 different Protestant denominations.

Vatican Council II encouraged ecumenism but made it clear that unity must always be based on truth and charity. Although Catholics cannot in good conscience compromise, change or water down their true faith, they can and must respect the sincerity of persons of different beliefs even when they cannot agree with them.

Catholics should show a genuine, deep concern for all who do not share their faith; but most of all, they should strive to live holier Catholic lives. By doing this, they will not only further unity but also put it into practice. Indeed, if all the members of the one Church Jesus founded had always lived according to the Gospels, Christians would still be united in the true faith. But it is not the fault of Protestant and Orthodox people today that such divisions exist. The separations occurred centuries ago. However, it is the responsibility of all Christians to remove the obstacles to unity by prayer, work and genuine Christian living.

At the Last Supper, Jesus not only prayed for unity among His followers, He even gave Himself to men in the Holy Eucharist to keep them one. God wills that the divisions among Christians cease. May Our Lord's prayer to His Father soon be fulfilled: "that all may be one, even as thou, Father, in me and I in thee; that they also may be one in us, that the world may believe that thou hast sent me" (John 17:21).

Christians throughout the world should be united under the Pope in the true Church. Instead, they are divided into hundreds of different kinds of churches.

REVIEW QUESTIONS

1. What is meant by "ecumenism"?

Ecumenism is a Greek word that means universal or worldwide. It has recently come to describe the movement toward greater understanding between Catholics and Protestants, between Catholics and Orthodox, between Orthodox and Protestants and between the various groups of Protestants, who have more than 400 different denominations. The word "ecumenism" describes the Christian Unity Movement in general.

2. May Catholics compromise their faith to obtain unity with other Christians?

No, Catholics may not compromise their faith to obtain unity with other Christians. Vatican Council II did much to encourage the Christian Unity Movement but stated that Catholics working for Christian Unity could not in good conscience compromise, change or water down their true faith. Unity must always be based on truth and charity, otherwise it is dishonest and insincere. However, this does not mean that there is no hope for unity; quite the contrary, for Catholics do share many common beliefs with other Christians.

3. Must Catholics respect the faith of other Christians?

Yes, Catholics must respect the faith of other Christians

even when they cannot in truth agree with them. Furthermore, Catholics should be deeply, personally concerned over the divisions among Christians. They can and should take the first steps to work for understanding and strive to be true to the faith they have received from Jesus and the Apostles. Catholics should pray for this intention and do all they can to further good will among Christians. Indeed, they should reach out to ALL people (including the Jewish race) who, with them, believe in God.

DISCUSSION QUESTIONS

1. Why are there so many different Christian churches in the world today?

2. Does Jesus will that Christians be divided? Explain.

3. Do Orthodox Christians have the powers of priesthood that Jesus gave His Apostles? Why?

4. How are the Eastern Rite Catholic Churches and the Western Rite Catholic Churches alike? How do they differ?

5. Name some common beliefs that Roman Catholics share with most Protestants.

6. Name some important practices or beliefs that Catholics and Protestants do not have in common.

7. Explain what is meant by the statement: "The Catholic Church has the FULLNESS of the true faith."

●●●

FOR OLDER STUDENTS

The mission given by Jesus to the apostles and therefore to the Church today is to bring all men to the gospel, to unity in "one Lord, one faith, one baptism" (Eph 4:5). This is because all mankind has been called by God's grace to salvation.

Baptized persons who are incorporated fully into the Church, and who possess the Spirit of Christ, are those who accept all the means of salvation Jesus gave His Church. This means Catholics who accept the entire organization of the Church, united by the bonds made up of the profession of faith, the sacraments, ecclesiastical government, and communion. These are joined in the visible structure of the Church of Jesus Christ, who governs through the Supreme Pontiff and bishops in union with the pope. This membership does not guarantee automatic salvation. One must also persevere in charity to be saved. One must be a member not only "in body" but also "in heart," said the Second Vatican Council. (LG 14).

The Church is joined in many ways to those validly baptized and are Christians but who do not profess the fullness of Catholic faith or have broke unity with the successor of Peter. These are in an imperfect communion with the Catholic Church. In the case of Orthodox Churches, they are very close to attaining the fullness that would permit a joint celebration of the Lord's Eucharist. Primarily, they would have to recognize the Pope as the supreme Pontiff.

The Church recognizes a certain relationship with the Jewish people. The Jewish faith is already a response to divine revelation in the Old Covenant which prepared for the coming of Jesus Christ and His Church. The Church sees a certain relationship with the Muslims as they also acknowledge the same Creator. They profess to hold the faith of Abraham and adore the same merciful God who will judge all on the last day.

The Church feels a bond with those of non-Christian religions as they have a common origin with us and are destined to the same end of the human race. These religions have often discovered some elements of God's goodness and truth and the Church recognizes this as "a preparation for the Gospel and given by him who enlightens all men that they may at length have life" (LG 16).

God the Father wills to reunite all mankind in His Son, Jesus Christ through His one Church. It is in the Church alone that mankind will find its unity and salvation. It is the obligation of the Catholic Church and its members to work and pray for that unity. Only in the faith of the Gospel can men please God. The Catholic Church then has both the serious obligation and sacred right to evangelize all men.

Catechism of the Catholic Church: 836-856.
Bible: Eph 4:5; Rom 1:21,25; 9:4-5; 11:29 Mk 16:16; Jn 3:5; Heb 11:6; 1 Cor 9:16.

Questions to answer:

1. Explain how one is a member in the visible structure of the true Church which Jesus Christ founded.

2. What more is required for salvation than formal membership in the one true Church?

3. What kind of union does the Catholic Church have with baptized persons who do not accept her visible structure and all that goes with it and what contributes to this kind of union?

4. Explain whether this kind of union (in the question above) with Christ's true Church is of the same value as full and formal membership in the Roman Catholic Church. Explain answer.

5. How does the Catholic Church regard the faith of Jewish people? The Muslims?

●●●

POINTS FOR PARENTS AND TEACHERS

Our American Bishops in Basic Teachings for Catholic Religious Education *state: "We recognize the unique fullness of the Catholic Church which we believe to be the ordinary means of salvation, and which we desire to share with all men. But we also recognize that Catholics can be enriched by the authentic insights into the Gospel as witnessed by other religious traditions.... Religious instruction is, then, to show a sensitive appreciation of the dignity and unique value of every human being. The Church rejects as un-Christian any unjust discrimination or injustice because of race, national origin, ethnic origin, color, sex, class, or religion. God has given to every man intrinsic dignity, freedom and eternal importance...."*

The Church teaches that Catholics are not to engage in inter-faith worship indiscriminately. Therefore, young Catholics should realize that specific permission from the bishop is needed for special inter-faith services. They should also understand that persons participating in Christian dialogue must be well educated and formed in their faith; otherwise, their dialogue will be superficial and possibly meaningless and false. For this reason, Catholics who are not rooted in the fundamentals of their faith are obviously not ready to dialogue effectively with other Christians.

Parents and teachers must be careful to present ONLY the official Church's teachings on ecumenism. They must also be sensitive that their manner of doing so does not create in youthful minds and hearts indifference to their own Catholic Faith. Usually young people do not have the experience and maturity to make adult distinctions, so these considerations are very important.

●●●

LESSON 28
THE MARKS AND ATTRIBUTES
OF THE TRUE CHURCH

In *Basic Teachings for Catholic Religious Education*, the Bishops of the United States said: "In the Catholic Church are found the deposit of faith, the sacraments, and the ministries inherited from the apostles....In the Church every individual has a call from God, a vocation to holiness. Each deserves respect, since all join in the one cause of Christ. The Pope and the bishops coordinate this work, in every rite, diocese, parish, and mission. In each, no matter how small or poor or isolated, 'Christ is present, and by his power the one, holy, Catholic and Apostolic Church is gathered together.' "

The American Bishops in *Basic Teachings for Catholic Religious Education*, the bishops of the world in *Vatican Council II* (1962-1965) and the Pope in the *General Catechetical Directory #66* all state that the Catholic Church is one, holy, catholic (or universal) and apostolic. These four marks have identified the Catholic Church as the true Church ever since it was founded by Jesus Christ almost 2,000 years ago.

The Catholic Church is One

The Bible speaks of "one Lord, one faith, one Baptism" (Ephesians 4:5). Jesus Christ founded only ONE Church.

Jesus wants but one flock and one shepherd.

Therefore, the Catholic Church all over the world must have the same teachings, the same sacraments and the same authority of Jesus in the Pope and bishops. Jesus gave His Church the Pope and the bishops under the Pope to keep it ONE. Since truth is one, people who say different things about a subject cannot all be right.

How many sacraments did Jesus give His Church? Does the priest have the power of Christ to forgive sins and change ordinary bread and wine into the Body and Blood of the Lord? Such questions can have only ONE true answer. Yet, hundreds of Christian churches disagree on these and many other important matters of faith. Jesus said He is truth (John 14:6). He also said that there should be only ONE flock and ONE shepherd (John 10:16). Therefore, on His word, all can believe that whoever rejects the Church Jesus founded rejects Him (Matthew 18:17 cf).

The Church is Holy

The Bible states: "...Christ...loved the Church, and delivered himself up for her, that he might sanctify her...that she might be holy..." (Ephesians 5:25-27). Now this does not mean that every Catholic is necessarily holy; rather, that the Church has the means to holiness and is, indeed, holy in many of its members.

The founder of the Catholic Church, Jesus Christ, is HOLY. All the teachings of the Church are HOLY, and the Church truly has the HOLY powers of Christ. It can forgive sins in Jesus' Name, give God infinitely perfect adoration in the Holy Sacrifice of the Mass and give grace through the seven sacraments. Rightly understood, the Church is HOLY because Jesus, its HOLY founder, is identified with it.

The Church is Catholic or Universal

In the Bible, Jesus said His Church must be worldwide (Matthew 24:14, 28:19-20; Mark 16:15; Acts 1:8; Romans 10:18). Truth does not change with time or place and is the same for ALL men. Furthermore, the one true faith must be for ALL men because Jesus died for ALL men. Our Lord truly wants persons of every race and nation to have the same faith with the FULLNESS of TRUTH as revealed by God.

The Church is Apostolic

The Catholic Church is apostolic because it has a history that goes back to the first APOSTLES upon whom Jesus built His Church with Peter as its head. This Church (founded on the Apostles) has not been destroyed and will never be destroyed. It will last for all time.

Jesus Christ gave the Catholic Church the FULL deposit of FAITH. This fullness of faith still exists and will always remain in the Catholic Church.

In addition to the four chief marks or signs by which men can recognize the Catholic Church as the true Church, Jesus also gave the Church three chief ATTRIBUTES or qualities: AUTHORITY, INFALLIBILITY and INDEFECTIBILITY.

All AUTHORITY (power to command) comes from God. However, Jesus Christ, the God-Man, has given His Church the authority to teach, to sanctify and to govern the faithful in spiritual matters in His Name. When Catholics obey the Church, they are truly obeying God because Jesus has said, "He who hears you, hears me; and he who rejects you, rejects me..." (Luke 10:16).

INFALLIBILITY means that Jesus has sent the Holy Spirit upon the Church to keep and guide it in truth whenever it teaches or believes a doctrine of faith or morals. Therefore, the Church, teaching through its head the Pope or the bishops of the world united with him, CANNOT err on doctrines of faith and morals. It has the power of Jesus to teach ONLY truth.

INDEFECTIBILITY means that the Catholic Church founded by Christ will never be destroyed.

It will last until the end of the world. The Catholic Church has had and always will have the truths and supernatural powers that Jesus gave it when He lived on earth.

REVIEW QUESTIONS

1. How do we know the Catholic Church is the one true Church established by Jesus Christ?

We know from history that the Catholic Church is the one true Church established by Jesus Christ. Jesus Christ founded only one Church, the Catholic Church.

2. How do we know the Catholic Church has the fullness of faith?

We know the Catholic Church has the fullness of faith because we believe that Jesus Christ is the Son of God and our Savior, and that the Church is the Mystical Body of Christ on earth. The Catholic Church alone has the four chief marks or signs by which all men can recognize it as the true Church.

3. What are the chief marks of the Catholic Church by which all men can know it is the true Church founded by Jesus Christ?

The four chief marks of the Catholic Church by which all men can know it is the true Church founded by Jesus Christ are: It is ONE, HOLY, CATHOLIC (or UNIVERSAL) and APOSTOLIC. No other church has ALL these four chief marks.

4. What are the three chief qualifies (or attributes) of the Catholic Church?

The three chief qualities (or attributes) of the Catholic Church are: AUTHORITY, INFALLIBILITY and INDE-FECTIBILITY.

5. What is meant by the Church's "infallibility"?

INFALLIBILITY means that Jesus has sent the Holy Spirit upon the Church to keep it in truth when it teaches or believes a doctrine of faith or morals. The Church teaching through the Pope or the world's bishops united with him CANNOT err on doctrines of faith and morals. They can only teach truth.

6. What is meant by the Church's quality of "indefectibility"?

INDEFECTIBILITY of the Catholic Church means that the Church Jesus founded will never be destroyed. It will remain until the end of the world. Furthermore, the Catholic Church will always possess the truths and supernatural powers Jesus gave it when He lived on earth.

DISCUSSION QUESTIONS

1. What are the four chief marks of the one true Church? Explain each.

2. Did Jesus promise that the Catholic Church would never be destroyed? Explain.

3. How can one prove that the Catholic Church is almost 2,000 years old and was the first and only Church Jesus Christ established when he lived on earth?

4. Name some Bible passages in which Jesus states that He

gave His Church the authority to teach, to govern and to sanctify in His Name.

5. What are the three chief attributes or qualities that Jesus gave to His Church? Explain each.

6. What does the word AUTHORITY mean?

●●●

"Where Peter is, there IS my Church.
Because Jesus chose Peter as the first Pope,
the Popes through the centuries have also been called "Peter. "

FOR OLDER STUDENTS:

One, Holy, Catholic, and Apostolic are four marks or characteristics of the Church which are inseparably linked with each other. The Church is not simply an organization possessing these four characteristics or marks of herself. There is the divine nature to the Church, making it a supernatural organism, as well as its human attributes. Jesus Christ is both human and divine. So is His Church. Jesus Christ through the Holy Spirit keeps His Church intact with these four characteristics. It requires the supernatural gift of faith to recognize these properties from their divine source in the Church.

The Church is One because her source, God, is one and there is one founder, "the Word made flesh." The Church is one because her Soul is the Holy Spirit who is the Spirit of unity.

The Church has a multiplicity of peoples and cultures. In spite of such great diversity from the beginning she has remained one in faith. Jesus gave the Church the pope who as an instrument of Jesus Christ through the Holy Spirit, would keep the Church in unity of faith and morals.

The Church is Holy - unfailingly holy. Why? Because Christ, the Son of God, her Head whose body she is, is holy and her soul is the Holy Spirit. Her members are often endowed with holiness however imperfect. Jesus came to call sinners so her members are sinners with the means to holiness. The Mother of the Church, Mary, is all holy.

The Church is Catholic, that is, universal. Her mission from Jesus Christ is to the human race of every nation and culture. She proclaims the fullness of true faith and bears the totality of means for salvation. By nature she is missionary and goes to all nations.

The Church is Apostolic because Jesus built her on the lasting foundation of "the twelve apostles of the Lamb" (Rev 21:14). Peter and the other apostles appointed by Jesus Christ are present in their successors, the Pope and college of bishops.

Attributes

Jesus gave His Church His own authority: In the discussion of the role of Pope and bishops in this Catechism, Jesus, Light of the World, the authority Jesus gave the Catholic Church has been demonstrated repeatedly. The Roman Pontiff and the bishops are the authentic teachers of the faith with the authority of Jesus Christ. St. Matthew closes his Gospel with Jesus saying: "Full authority has been given to me both in heaven and on earth; go, therefore, and make disciples of all nations" (Mt 28: 18-19).

Jesus gave the His Church the teaching authority of infallibility: The supreme degree of participation in the authority of Jesus Christ by the Church is ensured by the charism of infallibility. Jesus promised to be with His Church until the end of the world and that the gates of hell shall not prevail against it (Mt 16 17-20). This infallibility extends not only to the deposit of divine Revelation explicit in Sacred Scripture and its interpretation but also to the prescriptions of the natural law.

Proclaiming the natural law, as distinct from revealed law, is also part of the Church's prophetic office to teach the truth and lead men to what they should be before God and one another. St. Thomas Aquinas called the natural law "nothing else than the rational creature's participation in the eternal law" (*Summa Theologica*, 1a, 2ae, quest. 91, art 2).

St. Paul wrote of the natural law engraved on men's hearts, their own conscience, their own inner mental dialogue (Romans 2:4-15).

Jesus established His Church to be indefectible. Jesus promised that the gates of hell shall never prevail against His Church (Mt 16:19), and that He is Truth (Jn 14:6) and that His Church would be given the Spirit of truth to sanctify and keep it in the truth (Jn 14: 6,17; 15:26; 16:13 ; 17:17-19). To His apostles Jesus said: "He who hears you, hears me..." (Luke 10:16) and that "all power in heaven and on earth has been given me. Go.... I am with you all days, even unto the end of the world" (Mt 28:16-20). All this and more substantiates the Church's teaching that it can never be destroyed. The Church as the "body of Christ", mentioned repeatedly as such by St. Paul in Sacred Scripture, by its very nature being a divine organism, is indefectible.

Catechism of the Catholic Church: Marks: 811 - 870. Attributes: 2034-2038.
Bible: Marks: Jn 17:21; 11:52; Heb 7:25; Eph 1:4: 2:20; 5:25-26; Acts 9:13; 1 Cor 6:1; 16:1; 1 Cor 4:1; 2 Cor 3:6; 6:4; 5:20; 1 Jn 1:8-10; Mt 28:19-20; 2 Cor 5:15: 1 Tim 2:4; 2 Tim 1:13-14; Mk 3:13-14; Jn 5:19,30; 15:5; Rev 19:6; 21:9-14. Attributes: Mt 16: 17 -20; 28:18-19; Jn 14: 6,17; 15:26; 16:13 ; 17:17-19; Mt 28:16-20.

Questions to answer:

1. What is meant that just as Jesus Christ has two natures so His Church has two natures?
2. Explain the meaning of each of the four marks of the

true Church.

3. Explain the meaning of the divine attributes of the Church, namely, authority, infallibility and indefectibility.

4. What is meant by the natural law?

5. Why does the natural law, in addition to the divinely revealed law, also fall under the authority of the Church's authority to teach and lead men to be what they should be?

●●●

POINTS FOR PARENTS AND TEACHERS

Catholics must beware of a "false " ecumenism. They should not hesitate to teach emphatically that the Catholic Church ALONE has ALL four marks of the one true Church. It is neither honest nor charitable to water down the true faith or permit children to think that one church is as good as another. A committed Catholic must firmly believe that his Church alone has the full deposit of faith and all the powers that Jesus gave to His Church through the Apostles.

Parents and teachers should clearly and frankly present these facts to children. They should also encourage young Catholics to make converts so all may know and share the fullness of the true faith. In this way, the missionary spirit of the Church will he fulfilled.

LESSON 29
LIVING THE FAITH TODAY

At Baptism, God gives the soul sanctifying grace and enriches it with the supernatural POWERS of FAITH, HOPE and CHARITY. Throughout life, these POWERS, called VIRTUES, must remain living and constant and GROW.

By FAITH, Catholics know Jesus and His Church and believe all God has revealed and teaches in the one true faith.

The power of HOPE, which should also increase as one grows older, enables Catholics to trust in God's merciful forgiveness and His promise of everlasting life and happiness in heaven.

CHARITY is the virtue by which Catholics live God's great Commandment of Love: to love God above all things and all people for His sake. By the gift of charity, men love God and their neighbor with a SUPERNATURAL, not merely NATURAL, power.

Today some people mistake natural love, or liking, for the supernatural love which God pours into the soul by the power of the Holy Spirit. Charity gives Catholics the power to obey the Commandments of God and His Church even when they do not feel like doing so. Those who say they love God but refuse to follow His laws and those of the Church confuse SELF-LOVE with real love, which is supernatural charity.

Christians must have faith. By this free gift of God, they can truly meet, know and love Christ. Obviously they do not

The virtues of faith, hope and charity
received at Baptism
must continue to grow throughout life.

have to see Jesus with their bodily eyes, but they must see Him with the EYES of FAITH.

Jesus Christ is really alive and living today. He is present in souls by faith and grace and is truly present in the Most Blessed Sacrament. Through the powers of the priesthood, Jesus Christ continually comes and acts in our midst in a very special way. Catholic priests, who receive an indelible mark on their soul through the Sacrament of Holy Orders, have Jesus' POWER to offer Mass, change ordinary bread and wine into the Body and Blood of the Lord, forgive sins and administer other sacraments of the Church.

And why do Catholics believe these truths which the Church teaches? Because God has given them the POWER to BELIEVE. The ability to know, love, trust, meet and embrace Jesus as real and present comes from the power of the GREAT GIFTS of FAITH. HOPE and CHARITY.

The Apostle Paul states that no one can say in faith, "Lord Jesus" unless he is given the special grace, or power, from God to do so. Another Apostle, St. John, says all who believe that Jesus is the Christ have been begotten of God and have eternal life within their souls RIGHT NOW if they "...believe in the name of the Son of God" (I John 5:13).

When Catholics attend religion classes or listen to the Gospels or sermons at Holy Mass, they often see, in their mind's eye, Jesus, as He walks on water, brings the dead to life, cures the sick and lame, multiplies the loaves of bread, tells the stormy sea to be calm, etc. Now all these powers and deeds of Jesus are wonderful, but Catholics must not forget that Jesus continues to act and do even GREATER deeds TODAY.

For example, when a man goes to Confession, his sin-stained soul is made clean with the eternal life of Jesus. When

Catholics participate at the Holy Sacrifice of the Mass and hear the priest speak the solemn words of Consecration: "THIS IS MY BODY...THIS IS MY BLOOD," Jesus ACTS NOW as He did on the first Holy Thursday and Good Friday. And the very same Lord Who arose from the grave on Easter Sunday comes to Catholics in Holy Communion as the Risen Jesus. These tremendous happenings, which men are privileged to witness and experience, should fill their souls with great love, gratitude and humility.

How wonderful to believe, by the great gift and power of FAITH, that Jesus knows and cares for each human being, individually and personally. He knows, hears, sees and understands every thought, word and act and is pleased with all our efforts to overcome temptation and to do good. Indeed, there is nothing that escapes His infinite mind.

Yes, Jesus Christ lives and acts in many ways today. With the eyes of FAITH, Catholics and all Christians must learn to believe in Him, recognize Him, listen to Him and joyfully exclaim, "It is the Lord!"

Catholics can meet and experience Jesus in a very special way by receiving Him in Holy Communion.

REVIEW QUESTIONS

1. What is faith?

Faith is a power God gives to the soul. This gift, first received at Baptism, must continue to live and grow. By faith, Catholics meet and know Jesus Christ and His Church. This POWER enables them to believe all God has revealed and teaches through His Church.

2. What is hope?

Hope is another power God puts into the soul at Baptism. It, too, should grow stronger as one gets older. By hope, Catholics trust that God will keep His promises, forgive them their sins and bring them to everlasting life and happiness in heaven.

3. What is charity?

Charity is a power given at Baptism by which men can love God above all things and all other persons—not for any personal gain—simply for the love of God. The gift of charity enables men to love God and their neighbor with a SUPER-NATURAL, not merely a natural, power.

Today some people mistake natural love, or liking, for the supernatural love God gives to the soul by the power of the Holy Spirit. By charity, men have the power to prove their love for God by obeying His laws and the laws of the Church, even when they do not feel like doing so. People who say they love God but disobey His Commandments and refuse to follow the teachings and laws of His Church are confusing self-love with supernatural charity, which is real love.

DISCUSSION QUESTIONS

1. What gifts and powers does God give to the soul at Baptism? Explain each.

2. Is it possible for men to believe in God and His Son, Jesus Christ, by their own power? Explain.

3. Is a Catholic who claims to love God really loving Him if he deliberately and habitually fails to attend Holy Mass on Sundays? Explain.

4. Suppose a young Catholic habitually does many wrong things (such as: disobeying his parents, reading impure books, going to bad movies, etc.) but says: "These things are not sins because nobody gets hurt when I do them. Besides, I love God even when I do them." Does this Catholic really understand what it means to love God? Explain.

5. How do some people confuse self-love with real love?

6. Explain how Jesus is real and present in the world today.

7. Explain how Jesus is real and present in your own personal life today.

●●●

FOR OLDER STUDENTS

Man is called to the vocation of living in the Holy Spirit. There is a universal call to such holiness. The human person open to divine grace thus participates in the light and power of the Spirit of God. It is Jesus Christ who brings us this life and light. "In him was life, and the life was the light of men" (John 1:4). One who believes in Jesus Christ becomes a son of God. To live in the likeness of Christ one must develop firm habits or the human virtues. A virtue is a firm disposition to do good. A man of virtue has stable attitudes of the intellect and will that control his acts, order his passions with reason and faith. They are grouped around the four cardinal virtues: prudence, justice, fortitude and temperance.

Prudence directs the reason to make practical discernment for true good and choose the right means to attain it.

Justice consists in the will desiring to give God and neighbor their due.

Fortitude is a moral virtue that holds to firmness in difficulties and is constant in the pursuit of the good. It resolves to resist temptations and overcome obstacles to a good moral life.

Temperance moderates the attraction to pleasures of the senses and provides a balance in the use of created goods.

The human virtues can be acquired by education and acts repeated to become good habits which in the Christian life are then elevated by divine grace. The human virtues described above are rooted in the theological virtues of faith, hope and charity which are infused by God into the soul at baptism and dispose the faculties of man for participation in the divine nature.

The supernatural virtues of faith and hope remain even in

one who has fallen into mortal sin if the person does not sin against faith and hope. In fact they are needed to respond to actual grace to come back to sanctifying grace, the participation in the divine nature. Charity, the theological virtue by which we love God and our neighbor, is lost by mortal sin but restored by repentance. The sacrament of Reconciliation should be used to be restored to charity which always accompanies grace.

The seven gifts of the Holy Spirit are wisdom, understanding, counsel, fortitude, knowledge, piety, and fear of the Lord. They perfect the virtues of the one who receives them.

The fruits of the Holy Spirit are charity, joy, peace, patience, kindness, goodness, generosity, gentleness, faithfulness, modesty, self control and chastity. They are perfections by which the Holy Spirit is forming us for and gradually introducing us to eternal glory.

Catechism of the Catholic Church: 1700 - 1709; 1803 - 1841.
Bible: Col 1:15; 314; 4:1; 2 Cor 4:4; Phil 4:8; Wis 8:7; Prov 14:15; Ps 118:14; Jn 16:33; Jn 13:1; 15:9-12; Mt 22:40; Sir 5:2; 18:30; 37:27-31; Titus 2:12; Heb 10:23; Titus 3:6-7; Rom 4:18; 8::14; 13:8-10; 1 Cor 13:4-7; Gal 5:22-23 (Vul).

Questions to answer:

1. What is the call God gives to each one of us?
2. Explain each one of the four Cardinal virtues.
3. How are human virtues acquired?
4. What elevates these human virtues to a supernatural level?

5. Which of the theological virtues are lost by mortal sin?

6. Besides the theological virtues what else is given to the soul through the Holy Spirit?

•••

POINTS FOR PARENTS AND TEACHERS

The Bishops began Basic Teachings for Catholic Religious Education *by saying:*

"All religious education is formation in Christ, given to make 'faith become living, conscious and active, through the light of instruction.' Religious education is proclaiming to others the Gospel of the risen Lord, while showing that this 'Good News' alone gives meaning to life. So the faith, prayer and lived example of the teacher are of great importance.

"The sad fact is that many people today pay little or no attention to God, while others are persuaded that God is distant, indifferent, or altogether absent. That is because modern life is man-centered. not God-centered. Its climate is unfavorable to faith. Yet, no matter how hidden, some desire for God is lodged in every man."

Although parents are the PRIMARY educators of their children, they must work together with educators to help young Catholics develop a "living" faith. Jesus Christ, Our Lord and Savior, must be realized as REAL, PRESENT and ALIVE in the daily lives of all Catholics. His power, action and presence in the sacraments and Sacred Liturgy should be recognized and appreciated.

LESSON 30
A SPIRITUAL TREASURY

The kingdom of heaven has a SPIRITUAL TREASURY from which the Church draws special merits to help souls. This Spiritual Treasury contains the infinite merits of Jesus and the superabundant merits of the Blessed Virgin Mary and all the saints. It is like heaven's bank.

Jesus Christ is the cause and source of all merits. He alone has made infinite or perfect satisfaction for the sins of the whole world. (Merit means the right to a reward from God because of the performance of some good supernatural work.) However, Mary, the Mother of God, and the other saints have also gained merits by their prayers, sufferings and good works. These great Christians followed Jesus' teaching and example so closely that they earned more merits of satisfaction than they personally needed. In fact, the Blessed Virgin Mary had no need to make any satisfaction for herself because she NEVER sinned. She lived a perfect life, glorifying God and cooperating in the salvation of all her spiritual children.

Although the Spiritual Treasury contains the infinite satisfaction and merits of Jesus and the superabundant satisfaction gained by the Blessed Virgin Mary and the saints, it is ONLY through the power of Jesus' acts of redemption that Mary and the saints have been able to contribute to the tremendous spiritual storehouse from which all men can draw. Their superabundant merits make the Spiritual Treasury overflow, as it were, onto all God's people. And the Church, through the power given it by Jesus Christ, has the right to distribute these merits to penitent sinners and to take away temporal punishment due to sins that have been forgiven.

Men do not work out their salvation alone. They are united to Christ, the Head, and their fellow men, in the MYSTICAL BODY OF CHRIST, the COMMUNION OF SAINTS. Sin affects all members of the Church in the same way as all parts of the human body are hurt when one member is injured. By the same token, the whole MYSTICAL BODY is strengthened when one member of the Church grows in grace.

Some members of the Church offer many good works, prayers and acts of penance to God. By their virtuous lives, these Christians build up the Church's Spiritual Treasury and help make satisfaction for the sins of men. Thus, the COMMUNITY of the Church both builds up and draws from the common Spiritual Treasury of heaven.

Sometimes people who have lived in serious sin for many years suddenly come back to God. They receive the grace to be truly sorry for their sins and make a good Confession. Often such penitents do not understand how or why they were converted, but it was through the help of the entire Christian community. God in His love and mercy applied the merits of the Spiritual Treasury to them in their need. In eternity Christians will be able to understand this mystery. Then they will know exactly how and when they have helped or been helped by the good works, sufferings, prayers and sacrifices of others.

The Spiritual Treasury of the Church
contains the infinite merits of Jesus
and the superabundant merits of the Blessed Virgin Mary
and all the saints.

REVIEW QUESTIONS

1. What is meant by the "Spiritual Treasury" of the kingdom of heaven?

The Spiritual Treasury of the kingdom of heaven means the infinite merits of Jesus Christ and the superabundant merits of the Blessed Virgin Mary and all the saints. Jesus is the source of all grace and has made satisfaction for the sins of the whole world. However, all men who share in God's life in the COMMUNION OF SAINTS can indirectly or secondarily earn graces for others.

The Blessed Virgin Mary and the saints lived holy lives upon earth. They now intercede for us. By their prayers, sufferings and good works, these saints contributed to the Spiritual Treasury from which graces flow to the souls of men.

2. Does each person work out his salvation alone?

No, each person does NOT work out his salvation alone. Men are saved in and by Jesus Christ within the unity of His Mystical Body, the Church. People primarily need Jesus for salvation, but they also depend on other people or the Church Jesus founded. Our Lord has taught men to worship God as a community (Church) as well as to pray to Him privately. The people of God need each other. They especially need priests to teach and form them in Christ and give them the sacraments. They also need Mary, the Mother of the Church and Mediatrix of all grace.

3. Can men help save souls?

Yes, men can help save souls by their prayers, good works, sufferings and good example. In fact, they are obliged to do so.

Jesus Christ alone merited all grace. However, He wills that men help in His work of salvation. When the members of the Mystical Body, the Church, are holy, they have great power to intercede with Jesus, Mary and the saints for others. All men should pray, do penance and offer satisfaction to God for their own sins and the sins of the world.

DISCUSSION QUESTIONS

1. What is contained in the Spiritual Treasury of heaven?
2. What does the word "merit" mean?
3. Who made infinite satisfaction for the sins of all men?
4. Can men help save souls? Explain.
5. Does each person have to work out his salvation alone? Explain.
6. Did the Mother of God have to make any satisfaction for herself? Explain.
7. How is the Mystical Body affected by the sins and good works of its members?

●●●

FOR OLDER STUDENTS

We are not alone in the effort to purify ourselves, over-come sin and grow in grace so as to attain a greater share in the glory God has reserved for the saints in heaven. The life in Jesus Christ of each baptized person is joined in a wonderful way to the spiritual life of every other Christian. All form, as it were, one mystical person.

There is a union of charity of Christian souls on earth, with those in purgatory and those in heaven. In this holiness of the communion of saints, the holiness of one profits the other members of this communion far greater than sin of one harms others.

The spiritual goods of this communion of saints is called the Church's treasury. This treasury of the Church is of infinite value and the supply of its merits can never be exhausted. This treasury has the infinite merits of Jesus Christ and includes the super-abundant merits from the prayers and good works of the Blessed Virgin Mary and the saints of the Church.

Each one of us does not work out his salvation alone. We are members of the communion of saints which has that trea-sury of the Church with the infinite merits of our Brother, Jesus Christ, and the prayers and good works of millions of saints who drew from the merits of Jesus Christ.

The life of the Mother of the Church, the Blessed Virgin Mary, while she was upon earth, was exceedingly meritorious in virtue of her unique union with her Son, Jesus Christ. Now in heaven as advocate and mediatrix of all grace, she can especially dispense saving graces to us from her Son, who contains an infi-nite treasury of merits which God desires to bestow in, with and through Jesus Christ and the intercession of Mary and the saints. Even while Christ was the sole essential Mediator of grace, Mary had a certain role as mediatrix in union with and dependent on Jesus Christ while upon earth. From heaven where Jesus Christ is still our Mediator, Mary is our advocate and mediatrix in bestowing graces to those disposed.

The Catholic Church has been given the power of the keys of heaven. In the Church, sins can be forgiven through the power of the Precious Blood of Jesus Christ and the action of the Holy Spirit. Jesus, having died for us, wills that in His Church the gates of heaven always be opened for those who so desire admittance in repentance. The application of the infinite merits of Jesus Christ for the upbuilding of the members of the Church in grace and charity, drawing from the infinite supply of the Church spiritual treasury, is the prerogative of the Church. The Church, especially through the Pope, successor of St. Peter, was given the keys of the kingdom of heaven with the power to bind and loose and to dispense the grace of Jesus Christ. The Sacraments or liturgical life of the Church is the primary means of glorifying God and dispensing grace to souls and for the forgiveness of sin.

The daily prayers of the Church, such as seen in the "Liturgy of the Hours" and especially prayers and sacrifices of very holy souls, contemplative souls, even the prayers of the saints in heaven, are all available to everyone who is a member of the communion of saints. Throughout the Church Year the universal Church calls upon the intercession of the Apostles and special saints in heaven and even all the saints as is especially noteworthy on November 1st of each year. In the next chapter on "Indulgences" we will appreciate even more the value of this spiritual treasury.

Catechism of the Catholic Church: 981 - 983; 1474 - 1477.
Bible: Lk 24:47; 2 Cor 5:18; Mt 16: 16-20; 18:21-22.

Questions to answer:

1. How are we helped in being purified rather than accomplishing a life in Christ alone?

2. What is the Church's treasury?

3. How does each one of us benefit spiritually by being joined to the communion of saints in working toward our salvation?

4. How does the Church dispense to us from the infinite merits of Jesus Christ in the Church's spiritual treasury?

● ● ●

POINTS FOR PARENTS AND TEACHERS

This lesson will help young Catholics better understand and appreciate the following: Jesus as the Head of the Church and Savior of the world, the Church as the Mystical Body of Christ and the spiritual influence men can and should have on each other.

Young Catholics must be able to envision the Spiritual Treasury of heaven which contains the abundant spiritual gifts (graces) merited by Jesus Christ for all mankind by His life, death, resurrection and ascension. In truth, the Risen Christ is Himself that Spiritual Treasury.

Even children in the primary grades should be able to comprehend the Sacred Heart of Jesus, the total Person of Christ, as the Spiritual Treasury in heaven.

In explaining how the Blessed Virgin Mary and all the saints intercede for souls and how all men can also help and influence others, parents and teachers must emphasize that Jesus is the one essential Mediator Who has earned graces for all mankind. But, as

St. Paul says, the people of God must make up in themselves that which is lacking in the sufferings of Christ. In other words, the members of the Mystical Body can benefit from the Spiritual Treasury and also contribute to it by their good works, prayers, acts of penance and fervent Christian lives.

This lesson should assist parents and teachers in explaining the VERTICAL and HORIZONTAL relationship to God which has been expressed in other parts of this book. Vertical implies a direct relationship to God, but always in, through and with Jesus Christ. Horizontal means one's relationship to God TOGETHER WITH other members of the Church.

The vertical and horizontal beams of the Cross serve to remind Catholics that they must engage in both the horizontal and vertical approaches to God. A BALANCED SPIRITUAL-ITY consists of PRIVATE PRAYERS, GOOD WORKS, COM-MUNITY PRAYERS and SPIRITUAL ACTIVITIES. It means that Catholics are concerned about their own personal salvation as well as the salvation of others.

Jesus longs to have men come to His Heart
and receive the graces which flow from it
into the Spiritual Treasury of the Church.

LESSON 31

INDULGENCES

To understand indulgences, one must first understand the Spiritual Treasury of the Church. An indulgence NEVER takes away sin, but it does take away the PUNISHMENT due to sins that have already been forgiven.

God in His MERCY forgives those who are truly sorry they have offended Him; but His justice requires that SATISFACTION be made for the wrong done to the glory of the Blessed Trinity and for the injury done to the Church. In other words, satisfaction must be made for the offenses committed against God and His people. The Church through indulgences helps men do this.

Jesus Christ gave His Church the authority to grant indulgences. That means it can open the Spiritual Treasury (heaven's bank) and let the merits of satisfaction, which Jesus and the saints won for the remission of sins and the punishment due to sin, flow out to souls.

The Church has Jesus' power to forgive sins in the Sacrament of Penance. It also has His power to take away the temporal punishment due to sin, which remains after sins are forgiven. Catholics who gain indulgences will have less to suffer in purgatory because they have made satisfaction to God's justice.

The following examples may help Catholics understand

God forgives those who are truly sorry they have offended Him;
but His justice requires that satisfaction be made for sin.

the difference between the forgiveness of sin and the remission of the temporal punishment due to sin.

A boy who has deliberately broken a window may be forgiven by a kind, merciful person when he is sorry for his misdeed; nevertheless, justice requires that payment be made for the damaged window. Although indulgences have nothing to do with material possessions or money, they are, so to speak, "spiritual payments" made to God's justice for the harm caused by sin.

A forgiven sin can also be compared to a nail that has been pulled out of a tree. After both sin and nail are gone, a hole still remains. Indulgences are like putty. They "fill up" the holes caused by sins that have been forgiven.

There are two kinds of indulgences: PLENARY INDULGENCES and PARTIAL INDULGENCES. A PLENARY INDULGENCE takes away ALL temporal punishment due to sin. To gain a plenary indulgence, one must:

1. Do the work required by the Church.
2. Go to Confession.
3. Receive Jesus in Holy Communion.
4. Say some prayers for the Pope.
5. Be free from all attachment to sin, even venial sin.

Persons who die immediately after gaining a plenary indulgence would certainly go straight to heaven.

A PARTIAL INDULGENCE takes away PART of the temporal punishment due to sins that have been forgiven. To receive a partial indulgence, one must be in the state of sanctifying grace. Therefore, even those who have venial sins on their soul can obtain PARTIAL SATISFACTION for their sins by fulfilling the requirements of the Church for gaining a partial indulgence.

Catholics can gain partial indulgences by making spiritual communions, by devoutly using Scapulars and medals that have been blessed by a priest and by making INVOCATIONS while performing good actions. The following are a few of the many commonly used and highly indulgenced prayers recommended by the Church:

> "My Lord and my God."
> (This should be said especially when the priest elevates the Sacred Host and chalice at Holy Mass.)
> "Jesus, Mary, Joseph."
> "O Lord, increase my faith."
> "O Heart of Jesus, I place my trust in You."
> "Merciful Lord Jesus, grant them eternal rest."

PARTIAL INDULGENCES can be gained when Catholics: renew their baptismal vows, read the Bible, pray the Rosary or Litanies approved by the Church, teach or study Christian doctrine, visit the Most Blessed Sacrament, etc.

There are many occasions when Catholics may gain a PLENARY INDULGENCE. This is possible when they: attend the Good Friday Services and adore and kiss the Cross, recite the Rosary in the Presence of the Blessed Sacrament, make the Stations of the Cross, attend a mission and are present for its solemn closing, etc.

Those who fail to fulfill all the requirements for a plenary indulgence can at least obtain a partial indulgence. The satisfaction made to God depends on the degree of the person's faith, charity and sorrow. Any indulgence that can be gained for oneself can also be applied to the suffering souls in purgatory.

Indulgences are free gifts of God given through His Church. They bring an overflow of God's mercy to those who are sorry for their sins and perform an action to which an indulgence is attached. Such persons receive the remission of the temporal punishment which their own action merits, plus an ADDITIONAL, EQUAL remission through the intervention of the Church. In a sense, those who receive indulgences are like criminals who have been justly sentenced to a prison term but are freed after they have served only part of their sentence.

People who deny the Church's power to grant indulgences or consider them useless are in error. Pope Paul VI stated that the use of indulgences must be kept in the Church. He also reminded Catholics that indulgences have been authoritatively approved by the Sacred Councils.

Therefore, Catholics should always be grateful to God for the mercy and love He shows in granting indulgences. Furthermore, they should try to gain as many indulgences as they can, both for themselves and for the poor souls. God wills that men become completely united with Him in heaven. That moment can be hastened by those who use the Spiritual Treasury of merit gained by Jesus for souls.

●●●

REVIEW QUESTIONS

1. What is an indulgence?

An indulgence is the remission of some or all of the temporal punishment due to sins that have been forgiven. The Church, which has the power of the keys of the kingdom of heaven, grants indulgences.

God requires temporal punishment for sins to satisfy His justice. By means of indulgences, the Church takes away the temporal punishment due to sins already forgiven by drawing from the Spiritual Treasury which contains the infinite satisfaction made by Jesus and the superabundant satisfaction made by the Blessed Virgin Mary and all the saints. Christ gave His Church the power to distribute these merits to penitent sinners and to remit the temporal punishment due to sin.

2. How many kinds of indulgences are there?

There are two kinds of indulgences: partial indulgences and plenary indulgences.

A partial indulgence removes SOME of the temporal punishment due to sins that have been forgiven.

A plenary indulgence takes away ALL the punishment due to sins that have been forgiven.

3. What must one do to gain an indulgence?

To gain an indulgence, one must:

(1) Be in the state of sanctifying grace.

(2) Have the intention of gaining the indulgence.

(3) Do the work prescribed by the Church.

To gain a PLENARY indulgence, one must:

(1) Fulfill all the requirements necessary to receive an indulgence.

(2) Be free from all sin, even venial sin.

(3) Resolve never to sin again and to avoid the occasions of sin.

4. Why should Catholics work for the remission of temporal punishment due to sin by gaining indulgences? Is it not enough that they make satisfaction to God for their sins by doing good works of their own choosing?

Christians may and should perform good works of their own choosing in faith, love and sorrow in satisfaction for their sins. However, the meritorious value of good works to which the Church has applied a partial indulgence is more powerful than the value received from doing good works of one's own choosing because, in addition to the value of the good work itself, the Church applies an EQUAL remission through its intervention. That is to say, the Church draws from the Spiritual Treasury of Christ, the Blessed Virgin Mary and all the saints and gives a DOUBLE value to good works that carry an indulgence.

5. What happens to those who die in the state of "unforgiven" mortal sin?

Those who die in the state of "unforgiven" mortal sin must suffer eternal punishment.

6. What is meant by "eternal" punishment?

Eternal punishment means losing God forever and suffering in hell for all eternity.

7. What is the difference between eternal punishment due to sin and temporal punishment due to sin?

Eternal punishment will last forever. Those who die in mortal sin will lose God forever and be punished in hell for all eternity.

Temporal punishment will last for only a time. That means it will come to an end. Temporal punishment can take place either on this earth or in purgatory.

DISCUSSION QUESTIONS

1. Explain in your own words the meaning of indulgences.
2. Why is it necessary to understand the Church's Spiritual Treasury in order to understand indulgences?
3. Do good works to which an indulgence is attached offer

greater satisfaction for sins that have been forgiven than good works to which no indulgence is attached? Explain.

4. What is reparation?

5. Can one offer penance by giving up something that is permitted or good in itself? Explain.

6. Does the Church encourage its members to pray the Rosary in the Presence of Jesus in the Blessed Sacrament? Explain.

●●●

FOR OLDER STUDENTS

The Church's doctrine on indulgences is closely linked to the Sacrament of Penance. The effect of the sacrament of reconciliation when worthily received is the forgiveness of sin, while performing the penance which the priest prescribes at the time of confession is in reparation for sin being forgiven. It has the same effect as indulgences. Indulgences do not take away sin, just as the penance the priest gives does not take away sin. Both indulgences and the penance given to perform during the sacrament help remit the temporary punishment due to forgiven sin.

Every sin involves an unhealthy attachment to creatures. A mortal sin may be forgiven by a good confession and absolution but there is still purification needed for imperfections still in the soul. God in His love and mercy forgives mortal sin by a good confession through sacramental absolution and this takes away eternal punishment but this same God of love and mercy is also a God of justice. Justice requires that the sinner make reparation for having gone against the very purpose for which

God created him in His own image, namely to serve and give glory to the all good God. The sinner injures God's glory in the sense that one does not give glory to God when sin is committed but acts contrary to the purpose for which he was created.

It is not due to God's vengeance that He requires reparation, or that one must undergo temporary punishment in purgatory if one had not been perfectly purified from attachment to creatures in this life. It is rather the result of the very nature of sin itself. One must be completely converted away from any attachment to creatures and entirely purified before entrance into the eternal life of heaven.

The complete purification of the soul can be accomplished by bearing sufferings and trials God permits in our lives, doing works of charity and mercy, special prayers and acts of penance. The priest acts in the person of Jesus Christ and in the name of the Church when he gives one absolution at the time of confession. The penance the priest gives in this sacrament means Jesus Christ in His Church is commissioning this particular soul to do this particular penance for purification and satisfaction for the particular sins just confessed and for the temporal punishment due which will remain after the sins are forgiven. The Church is then at this moment granting absolution in the name of Jesus Christ through one of its priests and prescribing a kind of penance for further purification so that it need not be undergone in purgatory.

In the case of indulgences, the particular work has been prescribed by the Church through the Pope or bishop and has a special effect in purifying the soul, as the Church, with the power of the keys is drawing from the spiritual treasury of the Church. Since the Church with the keys, can remove the greater of the two consequences of sin, venial sin or even eternal punishment due to mortal sin, the Church also has the power of the keys to remove in full or in part the temporal punishment due to sin it has forgiven by granting of indulgences. For a soul to receive a plenary indulgence or full remission it must be free of all venial sin and have no attachment even to venial sin.

Catechism of the Catholic Church: 1471 - 1473.
Bible: Mt 7, 7-8; 26, 41; Lk 9, 23; 13, 5; 18, 1; 21, 34-36; Acts 2, 42; Rom 8, 13, 7; 12, 12; Eph 4: 22, 24; 6, 18; 1 Cor 9, 26-27; 10, 31; 2 Cor 4, 10; Col 3, 17; 4, 2; 1 Thes 5, 17-18; Jn 13, 15, 35; Acts 10, 38; Jas 2, 15-16; 2 Tim 2, 11-12; 1 Pt 4,13.

Questions to answer:

1. Do indulgences have anything to do with sin now on the soul?

2. What is the same effect that indulgences and the penance the priest gives us to perform have?

3. After eternal punishment is taken away by a good confession what still remains?

4. What association is there with purgatory regarding indulgences and the penance the priest gives when one receives the sacrament of Penance at the time of confession?

●●●

POINTS FOR PARENTS AND TEACHERS

To know and appreciate the doctrine of indulgences, it is necessary to understand the Church as the Mystical Body of Christ and the Communion of Saints as God's family. In studying indulgences, young people will come to a fuller understanding of:

- *God's mercy and justice.*
- *The power that Jesus gave His Church in the keys of the kingdom of heaven.*
- *The consequences of sin.*
- *The mystery of the Church.*

Young Catholics must realize that indulgences pertain only to sins that have been FORGIVEN and for which satisfaction must be made. Parents and teachers should make this unit practical by teaching students various indulgenced practices and then encouraging them to use these.

Pope Paul VI's Apostolic Constitution issued January 1, 1967, entitled The Doctrine of Indulgences, *is an excellent reference for parents and teachers to study when they are teaching a unit on indulgences.*

O my Jesus, it is for love of You, in reparation for the offenses committed against the Immaculate Heart of Mary, and for the conversion of poor sinners.

CONSCIENCE is a personal judgment as to whether something is right or wrong. Catholics are obliged to form their conscience correctly, according to the Commandments of God and the teachings of His Church. In matters of morals (right or wrong), they must accept guidance and be faithful to the teaching authority of God's Church. Those who do this can be certain they are following God's will.

The teaching authority of the Church, called the Magisterium, consists of the Pope and the bishops of the world who are in union with him. Catholics may not in good conscience obey anyone—parents, teachers, priests or bishops—who disagree with the teaching Magisterium of the Church.

Persons who try to live according to the teachings of Christ follow a "Christian morality" or way of life. Although it is not always easy to be a good Christian, God is pleased with those who try to live this commitment and rewards them with everlasting happiness in heaven.

Certain moral values are absolute. This means they do not change with time, place or circumstances. Christians must be willing to suffer and even give up their lives rather than violate or disregard such laws.

Even though God wants all men to know, love and serve Him, He does not force them to do so. Each person must use

*Catholics who wish to grow spiritually should make
a sincere examination of conscience every day.*

his FREE WILL and personally choose to accept or reject Jesus Christ. God is glorified when men freely respond to His will and love by obeying His Commandments and the laws of the Church.

Catholics who are striving for holiness of life examine their conscience every day, especially before retiring at night. This practice helps them know their failures and make proper resolutions for the future. It also prepares them for the general examination of conscience which must be made before receiving the Sacrament of Penance.

The following examen lists some duties young people have to God, to their neighbor and to themselves.

I.
I, the Lord, am your God.
You shall not have other gods besides Me.

Have I:
- Remembered to love and adore God each day?
- Prayed my morning prayers, evening prayers and other prayers of the day with attention and devotion?
- Studied my religion?
- Paid attention in CCD or Religion classes?
- Prayed for the suffering souls in purgatory?
- Been devoted to the Blessed Virgin Mary, the angels and saints and tried to honor them?
- Observed Friday as a day of penance?
- Tried to bring others closer to Jesus by my words and example?

II.

**You shall not take the Name
of the Lord, your God, in vain.**

Have I:

- Used God's Holy Name in a disrespectful or wrong way?
- Cursed or sworn?

III.

Remember to keep holy the Sabbath Day.

Have I:

- Missed Holy Mass on Sunday or a Holy Day of Obligation through my own fault? (Catholics may fulfill their Sunday Mass obligation by attending Mass on Saturday evening because the Lord's Day begins on Saturday night.)
- Been late for Mass through my own fault?
- Left Holy Mass early when I did not have an important reason for doing so?
- Worshiped in other churches and not in the Catholic Church?
- Been attentive, prayerful and reverent at Holy Mass?
- Made a good thanksgiving after Holy Communion?
- Done physical work or shopping on Sunday that was unnecessary or should have been done during the week?
- Used Sunday as a special day of rest, prayer and recreation, remembering that the ENTIRE day is the Lord's Day?

- Fasted for one hour before Holy Communion? (Water and needed medication do not break the Communion fast.)
- Gone to Confession before Holy Communion when this was necessary?

IV.
Honor your father and your mother.

Have I:
- Obeyed and honored my parents, teachers, priests and all in authority?
- Respected older people and been considerate and thoughtful of them?
- Tried to be kind to my parents?
- Offered to help around the house, yard, farm, Church or school?
- Been cheerful at home, school, etc., or have I been grumpy and refused to join in and cooperate with family projects and activities?
- Encouraged my family to pray together and taken part in family prayers?
- Respected my teachers and elders and never talked back to them?

V.
You shall not kill.

Have I:
- Become angry and lost my temper?

- Wished anyone evil?
- Fought with others, hit them or called them names? If so, have I apologized or tried to correct such behavior?
- Helped my friends and classmates at school in honest ways?
- Looked down on others who did not do as well as I?
- Been jealous of others?
- Tried to respect the feelings of others?
- Been kind to boys and girls who were lonely, poor or having a difficult time?
- Been kind and polite to everyone?

VI.

You shall not commit adultery.

Have I:
- Used bad or dirty words?
- Intentionally had impure thoughts?
- Gone to movies, watched TV shows or looked at pictures that were indecent, suggestive or immoral?
- Listened to or told dirty jokes or stories?
- Gone with bad companions?
- Taught others to do wrong or did what was wrong with others?
- Done impure acts alone or with others?
- Dressed immodestly?

VII.

You shall not steal.

Have I:

- Stolen or taken anything without permission? What? How much?
- Have I returned everything I have borrowed and paid back what I broke, stole, etc.?
- Harmed or destroyed the property of others?
- Always worked carefully and not cheated on time, etc., when I was being paid for a job?
- Cheated in school or in any other way?

VIII.

You shall not bear false witness against your neighbor.

Have I:

- Told lies?
- Harmed the good name or reputation of anyone by talking about them?
- Told secrets about others?

IX.

You shall not covet your neighbor's wife.

Have I:

- Looked at anyone in an unclean or covetous way?
- Prayed and thanked God for the holiness of marriage, for my parents and other husbands and wives?

X.
You shall not covet anything that belongs to your neighbor.

Have I:
- Been greedy, selfish or wanted unfairly what others had?
- Shared my possessions?
- Dominated or bullied others?

After making a good Confession, Catholics should be at peace because God in His mercy has forgiven them all their sins. They should, however, try to offer reparation to God by means of prayers, good works and sacrifices so that the temporal punishment due to sins can be lessened or completely taken away.

Catholics should
examine their conscience
each night before they go to bed.

REVIEW QUESTIONS

1. What is meant by conscience?

"Conscience is a personal judgment that something is right or wrong because of the will and law of God." *Basic Teachings for Catholic Religious Education.*

2. What is Christian morality?

"Christian morality defines a way of living worthy of a human being and of an adopted son of God. It is a positive response to God, by growing in the new life given through Jesus Christ." *Basic Teachings for Catholic Religious Education.*

If Christians respond to God in genuine love, the Holy Spirit gives them the grace and gifts to live according to Catholic Christian morality. However, Our Lord never intended that it would always be easy to live a moral life. He said His followers must take up their cross daily and follow Him.

3. Does Christian freedom mean that each person is free to follow his own personal opinions?

No, Christian freedom does not mean that each person is free to follow his own personal opinions. Rather, it means that men have a free will to accept or reject Jesus Christ and His teachings. Catholic Christians are obliged to accept guidance and instruction for day-to-day living.

The American Bishops state: "...the conscience of the Catholic Christian must pay respectful and obedient attention to the teaching authority of God's Church." *Basic Teachings for Catholic Religious Education.*

4. What is the "teaching authority" of the Catholic Church?

The teaching authority of the Catholic Church is the Magisterium which means the Pope and the bishops of the world in union with him. An individual priest, religious, parent or ANYONE who disagrees with the teaching of the Magisterium in matters of faith and morals, should NOT in good conscience be followed.

5. Do the moral values of good Christian living change from time to time?

No, the moral values of good Christian living do not change from time to time. The American Bishops have stated: "The Christian must know that there are moral values which are absolute and never to be disregarded or violated by anyone in any situation. Fidelity to them may require heroism of the sort which we see in the lives of the saints and the deaths of the martyrs." *Basic Teachings for Catholic Religious Education.*

DISCUSSION QUESTIONS

1. How can Catholic Christians form their conscience correctly?

2. What is the true meaning of the word "freedom" ?

3. Why should Catholics take time each night to examine their conscience?

4. What is meant by the Magisterium of the Church?

5. Are Catholics in good conscience free to follow those whose teaching is contrary to that of the Magisterium of the Church? Explain.

6. Name some Christian moral values that can never change.

7. Why can the Church rightly change the law on fasting before Holy Communion or eating meat on Friday but cannot change laws pertaining to divorce, purity, etc.?

FOR OLDER STUDENTS

Each time a person approaches the altar to receive the sacrament of the Holy Eucharist, namely the Body, Blood, Soul and Divinity of Jesus Christ in Holy Communion, he must first examine his conscience to see that he is in the state of grace. St. Paul made that clear in the Bible, 1 Corinthians 11; 17 - 34.

The sacrament of Penance for the forgiveness of sin requires that we first examine our conscience. All mortal sins must be confessed, even the most secret ones.

Moral conscience is within the inner heart of a person

where he discovers a law inscribed by God to do good and avoid evil. Conscience involves a judgment of reason and man is obliged to follow what he knows is right and just.

In forming one's conscience a person may never decide to do evil so that good may come from it. The end does not justify the means. Each person has to make moral choices. The conscience can either decide to make a right judgment in agreement with right reason and the divine law or to make an erroneous judgment departing from them. Our dignity as human persons requires that we form upright moral consciences. Prudent judgments about acts performed or to be performed requires perception of the right principles of morality according to the heart of God. Scripture tells us "God is greater than our hearts, and he knows everything" (1 Jn 3:19-20).

A person is obliged to obey the certain judgment of his conscience. To deliberately act against conscience is to sin. Sin is an offense against reason and truth. Sometimes moral conscience is in ignorance and makes wrong judgements about acts committed or to be performed. If one is ignorant of right reason and divine law through no fault of his own, the evil done by the person is not held against him. Still an erroneous conscience makes it no less an evil or disorder. One has an obligation to work to correct his conscience and work to become informed so as to form his conscience correctly and act rightly in the future.

What can lead to an erroneous conscience? The bad example of others, frequent exposure to immoral secular media, being enslaved by the passions, the mistaken idea that one can follow his conscience without the effort to discover what is the law of God and the teachings of His Church; lack of conversion and charity; being taught wrongly by others who incorrectly represent the Church's teaching on faith and morals. To refuse to study one's Catholic faith and go to trustworthy sources of those known to speak and teach in harmony with the Magisterium of the Church is not to be free of guilt. One is then guilty and therefore responsible for the ignorance. Perfect contrition is based on love of the all good God. Such perfect contrition of charity will remit venial sin and even bring forgiveness of mortal sin if it includes the intention to confess and receive sacramental absolution.

Contrition is imperfect if one sees the ugliness of sin or fears eternal damnation. This kind of contrition can obtain the forgiveness of grave sins in the sacrament of Penance.

A stirring of the conscience is a gift from the Holy Spirit which can lead to sacramental absolution. Seeking forgiveness of God requires first of all contrition, that is, sorrow of the soul and a detestation of the sin committed with a resolution to avoid the sin in the future.

Catechism of the Catholic Church: 1453 - 1458; 1776 - 1794; 1849.
Bible: Mt 7:12; 5-7; Rom 1:32; 2:14-26; 12-15; 1 Cor 8:12; 12-13; Gal 5; Eph 4-6; Lk 6:31; Tob 4:15; 1 Tim 5; 3:9; 2 Tim 3; 1 Pet 3:21; Acts 24:16.

Questions to answer:

1. What is required each time before one receives the sacraments of the Eucharist or of Penance?

2. What is an upright moral conscience?

3. Are we obliged to follow the prudent judgement of our conscience?

4. What is an erroneous conscience?
5. What can lead to an erroneous conscience?
6. When does one sin regarding conscience?
7. Explain perfect and imperfect contrition.
8. Why is the stirring of conscience a gift from God?

POINTS FOR PARENTS AND TEACHERS

Parents and teachers must help young Catholics form their consciences correctly. At an early age, children should learn that they have the obligation of forming a right conscience and that this cannot be done by merely following "opinion."

They must also be reminded and impressed with the truth that there are unchanging principles of morality. The official Church has stated: "There are moral values which are absolute and never to be disregarded or violated in any situation." (American Bishops' Basic Teachings for Catholic Religious Education.) *By this statement, the American Bishops are condemning new moralities or situation-ethics which falsely tell people that the teachings of God and His Church do not apply in certain situations. There is no reason for confusion or compromise in this matter because the Church's teaching is very clear.*

LESSON 33
A SPIRITUAL PROGRAM

Catholics should follow some definite, well balanced spiritual program if they wish to live their faith and grow in holiness. The 10-Point Daily Spiritual Program provides a practical plan to help Catholics of all ages advance in virtue and grace as they perform the ordinary duties of their state in life.

Although many of the suggestions in the 10-Point Daily Spiritual Program do not bind under sin, they provide an excellent examination of conscience for those who are striving to know, love and serve God more faithfully.

–1–
Sign of the Cross

The Sign of the Cross is a summary of the Catholic Faith. It should be the first act of each day.

–2–
Morning Prayers

Catholics should offer some prayers to God each morning.

My Morning Offering

🕇 My God, in union with the Immaculate Heart of Mary (here kiss your Brown Scapular...partial indulgence), I offer Thee the Precious Blood of Jesus from all the altars throughout the world, joining with It the offering of my every thought, word and action of this day

🕇 My Jesus, I desire today to gain every indulgence and merit I can and I offer them, together with myself, to Mary Immaculate... that she may best apply them to the interests of Thy most Sacred Heart. Precious Blood of Jesus, Save *us!!* Immaculate Heart of Mary, Pray for us! Sacred Heart of Jesus, Have mercy on us!

It is especially important that they include the Morning Offering. By this prayer, Catholics give every thought, word, action, joy and suffering of the day to the Sacred Heart of Jesus through the Immaculate Heart of Mary.

Many Catholics who wear the Brown Scapular of Our Lady of Mt. Carmel kiss it each morning. This simple but beautiful act is a wordless prayer by which they renew their consecration to Mary and express their love and devotion to her.

–3–
Aspirations During the Day

Aspirations are short prayers offered to God throughout the day which do not take away any time from daily duty or recreation. There are many occasions when Catholics can lift their minds and hearts to God by means of such fervent prayers.

The Church recommends many beautiful aspirations for its members to pray. Catholics are free to use those which are meaningful to them or else they may make up their own short personal prayers. Aspirations are a wonderful, practical means of praising God and living in His presence.

–4–
Daily Rosary

The Rosary is a powerful prayer which has been prayed by the faithful for centuries. Many Popes have recommended its use. In 1917, the Mother of God told the children of Fatima that people should pray the Rosary every day.

Whenever possible, families should pray the Rosary together. Catholics must try to meditate on the mysteries of the Rosary while they recite its vocal prayers.

–5–
Evening Prayers

Catholics should offer some prayers of praise, thanksgiving, reparation and petition to God each night before retiring. They should always remember to thank God for the graces of the day, examine their conscience and make a good Act of Contrition. They may also include any of their favorite personal prayers or "Church-approved" prayers in this last act of the day.

–6–
Spiritual Reading or Study

Catholics should do at least 15 to 20 minutes of spiritual reading or study each day. This practice will help them know, understand and appreciate their faith.

Students may consider CCD or Religion Class assignments as spiritual reading or study. They should always do this work in the spirit of prayer and remember to ask the Holy Spirit for His gift of understanding. It is better to read or study about God a little each day than to do so for a longer period of time ONLY once a week.

–7–
Sacred Liturgy

Catholics are obliged to attend Holy Mass every Sunday and Holy Day of Obligation. They should try to receive Holy Communion at least every Sunday, Holy Day, First Friday and First Saturday.

The Sacrament of Penance should also be received regularly, at least once a month and preferably every two weeks. Catholics must never delay going to Confession if they are in the state of serious sin. As soon as they feel they have committed a mortal sin, Catholics should try to make a perfect Act of Contrition and promise God they will receive the Sacrament of Penance as soon as possible.

Our Lady of Fatima requested that First Saturday Confessions and Communions be offered in reparation to her Immaculate Heart.

–8–
Angelus

The Angelus honors the Incarnation of Christ or God becoming Man. It is prayed three times a day—in the morning, at noon and in the evening. Church bells are often rung at 6 a.m., 12 noon and 6 p.m. to remind people to pray the Angelus. Many families like to pray this prayer together at meal time.

–9–

Visits to the Most Blessed Sacrament

Catholics should visit and adore Jesus in the Most Blessed Sacrament as often as they can, surely at least once a week. They should learn to talk to Our Lord, Who is present in the tabernacle of their Catholic Church, from their heart and make fervent acts of faith, hope, love, thanksgiving, contrition, reparation, etc., to Him.

Those who cannot make frequent visits to a Catholic Church should at least make a short visit to the Blessed Sacrament when they go to Confession or attend Holy Mass.

–10–

Lay Apostolate

It is not enough that Catholics know, love and serve God themselves. They must also help others do the same by their words, example and good works.

The lay apostolate consists in doing good for others. Catholics who wish to help their neighbor in need can do so by performing the Corporal and Spiritual Works of Mercy.

REVIEW QUESTIONS

1. What is the 10-Point Daily Spiritual Program?

The 10-Point Daily Spiritual Program is a plan of life which will help Catholic Christians grow in holiness as they practice their faith. This definite, well-balanced way of life will bring Catholics an increase in grace and strengthen their union with God in Jesus Christ through the intercession of Mary, the Mother of the Church.

Catholics who are faithful to the Daily Spiritual Program will obtain graces for themselves and for others.

2. If one adopts the 10-Point Daily Spiritual Program and then fails to keep some of its points, will he sin?

It is possible that a person who has adopted the Spiritual Program could sin if he failed to keep some of its points. But the matter of sin depends on what points were neglected and the frequency of the act or omission.

In other words, although there is no law from God or from the Church that says Catholics must follow every suggestion of the 10-Point Daily Spiritual Program, SOME of its points do bind under sin.

For example, if one were to go for a very long time, say a month, without any personal or daily prayers, he would be extremely careless in prayer and would, undoubtedly, be endangering his faith. This would certainly be matter for a serious examination of conscience.

The 10-Point Daily Spiritual Program given in this lesson is a reasonable program for the average Catholic.

DISCUSSION QUESTIONS

1. Why is a Spiritual Program of life necessary?
2. What points of the 10-Point Daily Spiritual Program should be followed each day?
3. Are there any points in the 10-Point Daily Spiritual Program that do not have to be practiced each day? Explain.
4. Name and explain the 10 points that make up the Daily Spiritual Program suggested in this lesson.
5. Do any points of the Spiritual Program bind under sin? Explain.

●●●

FOR OLDER STUDENTS

As Catholics we must: 1. believe the mystery of faith, 2. celebrate the faith, 3. live the faith, 4. develop a personal relationship with Jesus Christ in prayer.

In this Catechism, *Jesus - Light of the World*, we have presented the chief doctrines of faith and morals. Like the Catechism of the Catholic Church, which is for the whole world and dedicates at length its fourth Part entirely to Christian Prayer, so our final chapter is dedicated to prayer or living a spiritual program.

The Church first presents to us the mystery of the faith in the Apostles Creed. Secondly, through the sacramental liturgy, namely the Mass and sacraments, we celebrate our faith. Thirdly, we work to become conformed to Jesus Christ in the Holy Spirit to the glory of God the Father. The fourth and final step of prayer involves a spiritual program of living a vital and personal relationship with the living and true God. Prayer itself is traditionally defined as "the raising of the mind and heart to God." There are different kinds of prayer. We should request good things from God but one will lack much in his development in prayer-life if he does not advance beyond the prayer of petition. Prayer also includes adoration of God, blessing, thanksgiving, intercession and praise as well as reparation. When we participate at Mass we fulfill all these purposes of prayer.

Prayer, while primarily directed to God the Father, may also be addressed to Jesus Christ, who goes to the Father as Man on our behalf.

Prayer has different purposes or ends. Adoration is the first attitude we need in prayer, recognizing God as Creator. Petition prayer recognizes our need of God for all things, first of all forgiveness. The prayer of Intercession leads us to join ourselves to Jesus Christ the one essential Mediator. Jesus intercedes for us with the Father as does the Holy Spirit who "intercedes for the saints according to the will of God" (Rom 8:26-27). The prayer of reparation is directed to restoring relationships with God and neighbor to their rightful condition. It recompenses for the losses or harm caused by some morally bad action or intention. It means making up to God with greater love for the failure to know and love God for which we were created. The Sacrifice of the Mass is the infinite act of reparation which we offer in union with Jesus Christ Himself who offers what He offered on the Cross. Any good act can be offered in reparation or any prayer can be offered in reparation to God for offenses to Him or to His Blessed Mother, to holy persons or any neighbor. These must be offered in, with and through Jesus Christ.

The Holy Spirit as the Soul of the Church teaches and moves the children of God to pray as the Word of God is considered and the virtues of faith, hope and charity are expressed.

The greatest prayer is chiefly accomplished in the Holy Eucharist when the Church becomes fully what she is, one with Christ in offering Himself in sacrifice (and ourselves in Jesus) to God the Father in the unity of the Holy Spirit.

According to the Bible it is the heart that prays. If our heart is not in it, the prayer is in vain. Jesus taught us how to pray. From the Sermon on the Mount onwards Jesus insists on the conversion of heart if we are to pray rightly. Jesus, our Head, prays for us to the Father as our Priest and we pray in Him as members of His Body. We pray to Him as our God. Jesus said, "The Father and I are one" (Jn 10 30).

The only way we can truly pray, whether in private or communal prayer, is if we pray in the name of Jesus. The human nature of Jesus is the way by which the Holy Spirit teaches us to pray to God our Father.

The Church invites us to daily prayer. The Liturgy of the Hours and the Holy Eucharist, especially on Sundays and feasts of the liturgical year, involves the official prayers of the Church and therefore of Christ praying in the Church and the members praying in Christ.Prayer may be vocal, (body and soul); mental prayer (interior acts of the mind and affections) which may be simple meditation (thought, emotion, desire) or the prayer of contemplation (achieving union with the prayer of Jesus and sharing in His mysteries). We live as we pray since we pray as we live. Temptations to distraction and dryness need to be fought with faith, trust, conversion and vigilance of heart.

When the Lord taught "The Lord's Prayer" He was not giving a formula to be repeated mechanically but the model of perfect prayer. In it Jesus presented us all the fundamental aspirations to be included in prayer. The Lord's Prayer is the summary of the whole gospel and the center of the Scriptures.

The Church employs he Lord's Prayer as an integral part of the praying the Liturgy of the Hours and the sacraments of initiation: Baptism, Confirmation and Holy Eucharist.

The first three petitions of the Our Father are directed to the glory of the Father. The four others present our needs.

Each Catholic should develop a habit of having a spiritual program consisting of definite exercises of prayer on a daily, weekly or monthly basis. While the spirit of prayer should always be in one's heart, it will not be there unless one develops a rule of life that consists of some spiritual program that is practiced regularly.

Catechism of the Catholic Church: 2558 - 2856.
Bible: Ps. 130:1; Lk 7: 36-50; 11:13; 18:9-4; 19: 1-10; Acts 17:27; Heb 10:5-7; Mt 5:23-24; 44-45; 6:7; 9-13: 25-26; 26:41: Mk 9:23; 10:22; 11:24; 14:36; Jn 14: 16-17: 23-26; Eph 1:3-14; 2 Cor 1:3-7; 1 Pet 1:3-9; Rom 8:16, 22-26, 34; 15:30; 16: 25-27; Jude 24-25; Rev 18:24; 19: 1-8; Col 4:2,12; 1 Jn 2:1; 1 Tim 2:5-8; 1 Thess 5:188; Ps 40:2; Song 1:7; 3:1-4; Jer 31:33; Eph 3:16-17;

Questions to answer:

1. Can the mystery of our faith be living and of value if we do not develop a personal relationship with Jesus Christ? Explain answer.

2. State what is missing if one's concept of prayer is simply petitioning God for things one desires.

3. What is the first attitude we need in prayer and what does it involve?

4. State some different kinds of prayer.

5. What are the two divisions of the seven petitions contained in the Lord's Prayer?

●●●

POINTS FOR PARENTS AND TEACHERS

Parents and teachers often fail to teach prayer in a practical manner. They should help young Catholics realize that spiritual duties are an essential part of everyday living.

The total Catholic Christian commitment must be integrated into a workable, unified program so that young people will include all the important practices of their faith into their daily lives and not merely concentrate on a few.

Often when one phase of Christian duty is being taught, young Catholics tend to think about it exclusively and forget about other practices of equal or greater importance. However, if they are presented with a total program, they will better understand how the faith, which is made up of various parts, can be implemented into a complete, practical, daily way of life.

The 10-Point Daily Spiritual Program is suitable for Catholics of all ages and readily adapts to every plan of spirituality, including the Apostolate of Prayer. Because the Spiritual Program is so important, it must not be mentioned only once. Rather, it should be reviewed, expanded and developed by continuous instruction and personal examination throughout the year.